S J B

W9-APY-223

Peer Support Strategies

for Improving
All Students'
Social Lives
and Learning

Peer Support Strategies

for Improving All Students' Social Lives and Learning

by

Erik W. Carter, Ph.D.
University of Wisconsin–Madison

Lisa S. Cushing, Ph.D., BCBA
University of Illinois at Chicago

and

Craig H. Kennedy, Ph.D., BCBA
Vanderbilt University
Nashville, Tennessee

Baltimore • London • Sydney

Paul H. Brookes Publishing Co.
Post Office Box 10624
Baltimore, Maryland 21285-0624
USA

www.brookespublishing.com

Copyright © 2009 by Paul H. Brookes Publishing Co., Inc.
All rights reserved.

"Paul H. Brookes Publishing Co." is a registered trademark of
Paul H. Brookes Publishing Co., Inc.

Manufactured in the United States of America by
Victor Graphics, Inc., Baltimore, Maryland.

The individuals described in this book are composites based on the authors' experiences. In all instances, names and identifying details have been changed to protect confidentiality.

Purchasers of *Peer Support Strategies for Improving All Students' Social Lives and Learning* are granted permission to photocopy the blank forms in the appendix for educational purposes. None of the forms may be reproduced to generate revenue for any program or individual. Photocopies may only be made from an original book. *Unauthorized use beyond this privilege is prosecutable under federal law.* You will see the copyright protection notice at the bottom of each photocopiable page.

Library of Congress Cataloging-in-Publication Data

Carter, Erik W.
  Peer support strategies for improving all students' social lives and learning / by Erik W. Carter, Lisa S. Cushing, Craig H. Kennedy.
    p.   cm.
  Includes bibliographical references and index.
  ISBN-13: 978-1-55766-843-1 (pbk.)
  ISBN-10: 1-55766-843-4 (pbk.)
  1. Peer counseling of students.   2. Students with disabilities—Education.   I. Cushing, Lisa S.   II. Kennedy, Craig H.   III. Title.
LB1027.5.C39625 2009
371.4'047—dc22   2008038459

British Library Cataloguing in Publication data are available from the British Library.

2012   2011   2010   2009   2008

10   9   8   7   6   5   4   3   2   1

Contents

About the Authors

Erik W. Carter, Ph.D., Assistant Professor of Special Education, University of Wisconsin–Madison, 432 East Campus Mall, Madison, Wisconsin 53706

Dr. Carter's research, teaching, and writing focus on effective strategies for including youth and young adults with disabilities meaningfully in schools and communities. He is the author of *Including People with Disabilities in Faith Communities: A Guide for Service Providers, Families, and Congregations* (Paul H. Brookes Publishing Co., 2007) and co-author of *Peer Buddy Programs for Successful Secondary School Inclusion* (Paul H. Brookes Publishing Co., 2008) and *The Transition Handbook: Strategies High School Teachers Use That Work!* (Paul H. Brookes Publishing Co., 2000). Prior to receiving his doctorate from Vanderbilt University, he was a high school transition teacher in San Antonio, Texas.

Lisa S. Cushing, Ph.D., BCBA, Associate Professor, Department of Special Education, University of Illinois at Chicago (UIC), 3233 EPASW, 1040 West Harrison Street, Chicago, Illinois 60607

Dr. Cushing holds a doctorate in special education from the University of Oregon. Before her tenure at UIC, Dr. Cushing served as a Research Assistant Professor in the Department of Special Education of Peabody College at Vanderbilt University and an Assistant Research Professor at the Center for Autism and Developmental Disabilities at the University of South Florida. She has published more than 20 journal articles and book chapters in the areas of peer supports, social interaction, instructional supports, access to the general education, transition, secondary education, inclusion, technical assistance, and positive behavior supports. She sits on the editorial board for *The Journal of Positive Behavior Interventions*. Prior to working in academia, Dr. Cushing was a special educator for students with significant disabilities in Hawaii.

Craig H. Kennedy, Ph.D., BCBA, Chair, Special Education Department, and Professor of Special Education and Pediatrics, Box 328, Peabody College, Vanderbilt University, Nashville, Tennessee 37203

Dr. Kennedy is Chair of the Special Education Department and Professor of Special Education and Pediatrics at Vanderbilt University and is a Vanderbilt Kennedy Center Investigator. He also is Director of the Vanderbilt Kennedy Behavior Analysis Clinic. Dr. Kennedy received a master of science degree in special education and rehabilitation from the University of Oregon and a doctorate in special education with an emphasis in quantitative sociology from the University of California, Santa Barbara.

Dr. Kennedy has published more than 140 scholarly works, including the book *Single-Case Designs for Educational Research* (Allyn & Bacon, 2005). He has served as Associate Editor of the *Journal of Applied Behavioral Analysis*, *Journal of Behavioral Education*, and *Journal of The Association for Persons with Severe Handicaps*.

He is a Board Certified Behavior Analyst and Secretary of the Board of Trustees of the Society for the Experimental Analysis of Behavior. He is a member of the American Association on Intellectual and Developmental Disabilities, Association for Behavior Analysis, Society for Neuroscience, and TASH. He also serves on the editorial boards of many highly respected peer-reviewed journals.

In 1991, Dr. Kennedy received TASH's Alice H. Hayden Award, and in 1993, he received the B.F. Skinner New Research Award from the American Psychological Association, Division 25. He was also recognized in 2003 for his research excellence by Peabody College at Vanderbilt University.

Preface

When asked about their memories of middle and high school, most people are quick to speak about their friendships and the experiences they shared alongside their peers. Conversations about school often include stories about best friends, favorite hangouts, lunchtime spent with peers, time spent together between classes and before school, participation in extracurricular and after-school activities, and involvement in other social events. Indeed, schools provide a rich and supportive context for children and youth to get to know, learn alongside, mutually support, and develop relationships with one another. These relationships can bring a sense of enjoyment, promote engagement in school, and influence the overall quality of life that students experience.

Schools also have a profound influence on student learning, shaping the ways youth view the world and are viewed by others. Middle and high school represents a critical juncture during which youth acquire the skills, knowledge, and attitudes that equip them to assume valued roles in their schools, homes, and communities—both during adolescence and into adulthood. Participation in a broad range of academic and elective classes, school activities, and extracurricular offerings provides a context for students to expand their interests, explore new worlds, become more self-determined, and broaden their experiences. Collectively, these learning opportunities shape the goals and aspirations of youth as they look ahead to life after high school.

At the same time, the absence of meaningful social relationships can leave an indelible mark on a person. When a sense of belonging remains elusive for students, when they have few supportive relationships to which they can turn, or when they are socially disconnected from others within the larger community of learners, the long-term impact on the lives of youth can be profound. Social isolation, being bullied, and the absence of positive relationships are all strongly linked to negative outcomes during adolescence and throughout adulthood. Furthermore, too many students still leave school without the skills, opportunities, and learning experiences needed to live the kinds of lives they aspire to. They may participate in a narrow range of classes, access only a small portion of the general curriculum, or receive relatively few of the supports needed to achieve to their potential.

The social and learning opportunities that schools provide to students really do matter. Yet, too many students with severe disabilities miss out on these important learning experiences and peer relationships because they lack appropriate supports or are afforded insufficient opportunities. Despite broad recognition of the importance of promoting inclusion, access to the general curriculum, and high expectations for students with severe disabilities, the potential social and academic benefits available within inclusive classrooms do not accrue for far too many middle and high school students with severe disabilities. It is becoming increasingly evident that how we support students to participate in classrooms and school activities must receive at least as much consideration as where students are served.

This book is focused on improving the social lives and learning opportunities of students with and without disabilities. We have written this book to equip teachers, paraprofessionals, and school staff with effective strategies to assist students with severe disabilities to access rigorous, relevant learning experiences and to enjoy meaningful relationships with their peers.

In Chapter 1, we highlight some of the ways that service delivery and educational programs have evolved for students with severe disabilities. Recent legislative, research, and school reform efforts are calling on schools to think differently about where students with severe disabilities should spend their school days, what they should be expected to learn, and who they should learn it with. Indeed, every student should have meaningful opportunities to learn important curricular content; develop valued relationships with their classmates; and experience the full range of social, learning, and other opportunities that exist within their schools and communities. We discuss how these emerging developments represent a substantial leap forward in the experiences and outcomes that schools, families, and communities should expect for students with severe disabilities.

An emphasis on evidence-based practices has risen to the forefront of discussions surrounding special education and transition services. This emerging focus represents a fundamental shift in factors expected to inform educational decision making for students with disabilities, challenging 1) researchers to develop intervention strategies characterized by clear evidence of efficacy and feasibility and 2) educators to draw upon and implement those strategies with fidelity and consistency. In Chapter 2, we introduce peer support arrangements as an educational practice that combines practical, flexible strategies with strong research support. We describe how, in addition to providing an effective alternative to individually assigned paraprofessionals and teachers, peer support strategies have been shown to improve the academic engagement and social interactions of students with and without disabilities.

In Chapter 3, we emphasize collaborative teaming as the foundation for successful inclusion. Peer support strategies will have the greatest impact when general educators, special educators, and paraprofessionals work together to plan how students will access the general curriculum, work together, and exchange support with one another. In many schools, this may require educational teams to explore new ways of working together to deliver effective instruction and supports. We describe practical steps teams can take to craft meaningful support plans for enhancing the academic and social participation of students with severe disabilities in general education classrooms. We also highlight the importance of ensuring that the learning experiences of students align with those of their classmates.

Peer relationships play an important role in the lives of adolescents. And, peer support strategies are often recommended as a promising avenue through which new relationships might form and grow. Chapter 4 highlights the importance of identifying students who are likely to work well together in ways that are mutually beneficial and promote reciprocal relationships. Although there is no single "formula" for promoting friendships, we present several factors educators might consider when identifying students with and without severe disabilities who will participate in these educational interventions. Because it is essential to ensure that the preferences and choices of students are considered, we emphasize the importance of actively involving students in deciding how, where, and from whom they will receive support.

In Chapter 5, we present practical steps educators can take to equip students to provide academic and social support effectively to their classmates. To prepare students to assume these new responsibilities with confidence and competence, we recommend setting aside time to orient participating peers to their roles by providing them with the information, skills, and strategies they will need to make these arrangements successful. These initial orientation sessions also offer an opportune time for educators to establish roles and interactions among students that enhance, rather than inhibit, the development of real friendships. The guidance that educators provide and the interactions they model have an important influence on the relationships that are likely to emerge.

As students work together, they will exchange an array of practical supports, learn important skills, participate more fully in class activities, meet new classmates, and develop lasting relationships. In Chapter 6, we discuss some of the ways that educators and paraprofessionals can help launch peer support arrangements with a strong start so that these experiences emerge. A variety of strategies exist for promoting collaborative work and encouraging social interactions. Although educators should be actively involved in monitoring students and providing feedback, steps should also be taken to gradually fade back the direct support provided by adults. We offer two illustrations of peer support arrangements in action and encourage readers to consider how these strategies might be implemented in their own schools.

In Chapter 7, we turn to the important task of reflecting on the progress that students with and without disabilities are making as they participate in peer support arrangements. Effective teachers regularly gather data on student performance and the broader impact of their intervention efforts, reflect carefully on those findings, and adjust their instructional programs and supports accordingly. We illustrate a variety of approaches that teachers can use to determine whether and how students are benefiting academically, socially, and behaviorally from peer support strategies. In addition, we discuss how this information can be used to tailor peer support arrangements to maximize their impact and acceptability to students and staff.

We conclude this book with a look toward the near future. Although much progress has been made in improving the quality of educational services and supports for students with severe disabilities, there is much still to do. The fact that you are reading this book suggests that you are a fellow traveler in this important journey. We hope that this book will be a practical resource as you do the important work of improving the social lives and learning opportunities of students with severe disabilities.

Acknowledgments

Like most other aspects of life, research is best undertaken as a collaborative endeavor. Such an approach has certainly characterized our work. We want to acknowledge the efforts of the many individuals who have worked on our research projects addressing peer support interventions and inclusion, including Zainab Al-Khabbaz, Lissa Brown, Dana Brickham, Nitasha Clark, Sierra Dillaway, Liz Gilliam, Jennifer Fey, Moira Finnefrock, Kristin Hasselbacher, Faye Irving, Julie Kiehl, Colleen Kurkowski, J.J. Longley, Linda Maeda, Macid Melekoglu, Sarah Moore, Cindy Nash, Soon-Jin Oh, Tae-Hoon Oh, Smita Shukla, Lynn Sisco, Beth Swedeen, Terry Wallace, Sanford Watanabe, Joni Wong, Jane Yanagida, and Vicky Zimmerman. We are especially grateful for the numerous teachers and administrators at schools in California, Hawaii, Pennsylvania, Tennessee, and Wisconsin who graciously opened their classrooms and partnered with us on these various research studies. We continue to be encouraged and amazed by the work you are doing to improve the educational experiences of all students in your schools.

We could not have undertaken these research projects or written this book without the generous financial support of the U.S. Department of Education, Office of Special Education Programs (Grants H086D40009, H324D020009, H325D000026, and H326C990016); the University of Hawaii, Office of Research Administration; the Wisconsin Alumni Research Foundation; and the Centers for Medicare & Medicaid Services, Medicaid Infrastructure Grant to the Wisconsin Department of Health Services (CFDA No. 93.768).

Finally, we would like to express a special word of appreciation to the editorial and production teams at Paul H. Brookes Publishing Co., including Rebecca Lazo, Steve Plocher, and Mika Smith. The high-quality resources you consistently publish are making a real difference in the lives of children with disabilities and their families. We are thrilled to have the opportunity to partner again with such fine colleagues in this important work.

To Robert Gaylord-Ross and Tom Haring

Peer Support Strategies

for Improving
All Students'
Social Lives
and Learning

1

Social Relationships, Inclusion, and Access to the General Curriculum

An impressive array of educational strategies is now available for teaching students with severe disabilities (Kennedy & Horn, 2004; Ryndak & Alper, 2002; Snell & Brown, 2006; Westling & Fox, 2004). Academics, communication, daily living, employment, self-determination, and social interaction represent just a sampling of the range of important domains in which effective instructional and support strategies have been developed, tested, and refined. These evidence-based interventions have brought into reach many abilities and opportunities students with severe disabilities, their families, friends, and teachers previously considered unattainable. In a relatively short time, expectations for students with severe disabilities have increased dramatically and these aspirations continue to rise.

An exemplar of these advances over just a few decades is our understanding and ability to facilitate *social interactions*. Prior to discussing developments in the social interaction literature, however, we want to briefly talk about how, as a field, we arrived at a place in which we can discuss educational gains, not just in instructional techniques but also in the learning opportunities that in the past seemed only a distant hope. It is because of these foundations that the intervention literature relating to social interaction has been able to develop and flourish. Therefore, it is worth taking the time to discuss these developments so that we can appreciate how far we have come, before we talk about how far we can go.

A HISTORY OF EDUCATIONAL INTERVENTIONS FOR STUDENTS WITH SEVERE DISABILITIES

Educational interventions for students with severe disabilities have a relatively long history (Kennedy, 2005). The formal development of curriculum and intervention strategies for students with severe disabilities began with the work of Jean-Marc-Gaspard Itard in France in the early 1800s. Itard—working with Victor, the "wild boy of Aveyron"—developed the first systematic instruction techniques and focused on language development and daily living skills (Lane, 1976). Itard's work—and Victor's gains—demonstrated that a person with significant developmental disabilities could learn through carefully designed and tested teaching techniques. This initial work was furthered by Edouard Séguin (1856), a protégé of Itard who established the first schools for individuals with severe disabilities. This work was carried forward into the early 20th century by Maria Montessori (1912), who extended these techniques for working with typically developing children.

In America, Paul Fuller (1949), a student of the famous behaviorist B.F. Skinner, began translating basic behavioral mechanisms discovered in the laboratory into ways of modifying the behavior of people with the most significant disabilities. Fuller's work suggested not only that people with profound, multiple disabilities were capable of benefiting from education but also that a system of instruction could be developed based on fundamental principles of learning. This work was quickly followed by a flurry of research that helped lead to the development of applied behavior analysis in the 1960s (Baer, Wolf, & Risley, 1968). In particular, Ferster and DeMyer (1961) and Wolf, Risley, and Mees (1964), working with children with autism, and Bijou and Baer (1961), studying typical child development, further established the utility of systematic instruction as a teaching tool.

Since the 1990s, we have seen a further evolution of the notion of curriculum in two principal areas: access to the general curriculum and social relationships.

This work in the mid-20th century in the United States, however, focused primarily on instructional techniques and did not explicitly address the issue of curriculum (Wolfensberger, 2008). That is, what is it that we should be teaching children with disabilities? The passage of the Education for All Handicapped Children Act of 1975 (PL 94-142) forced educators to consider this issue more closely. PL 94-142 required public schools to provide an education to all children, including those with severe disabilities (Trent, 1994). Prior to the passage of this federal law, many states and school districts did not provide educational opportunities for students with severe disabilities. Once this law was enacted, however, schools needed to decide what to teach students and, because few precedents existed, it was not entirely clear what this focus should be. After much discussion among educators and advocates, an important movement emerged in the field of severe disabilities to teach functional life skills within the context of a life-span approach (Brown, Branston, Hamre-Nietupski, Pumpian, et al., 1979; Brown et al., 1980). This approach to curriculum was very logical, focusing on daily living and work skills within the framework of successful adult functioning in the community. This new curricular emphasis was integrated into existing strategies of systematic instruction and produced a voluminous body of evidence-based practices for educating students with severe disabilities (Cipani & Spooner, 1994; Wehmeyer & Patton, 1999). Although this emphasis was life-span–oriented and functional—both major improvements in curriculum—there was some disconnect between an adult-oriented curriculum and students who were attending elementary and secondary schools. In particular, there was a perceived gap between the curriculum for students without disabilities and the curriculum being provided to students with severe disabilities (Downing, 2005c; Spooner, Dymond, Smith, & Kennedy, 2006; Turnbull, Turnbull, Wehmeyer, & Park, 2003).

Thus, since the 1990s, we have seen a further evolution of the notion of curriculum in two principal areas: access to the general curriculum and social relationships (see Behind the Strategies on p. 3). The emphasis on access to the general curriculum has emerged for several reasons, including recognition of the need to 1) better align curricular content for students with and without disabilities, 2) contextualize skill development within a broader curricular format,

3) foster greater membership in general education classes, and 4) facilitate access to general education class materials and activities for students with severe disabilities (Browder, Spooner, Wakeman, Trela, & Baker, 2006; Carter & Kennedy, 2006; Spooner et al., 2006). The result has been an increase in the regular class participation of students with severe disabilities and a greater degree of alignment between individualized education program (IEP) goals and the general curriculum (Browder & Spooner, 2006; Williamson, McLeskey, Hoppey, & Rentz, 2006).

This emphasis on the general curriculum as the central focus of instruction for students with severe disabilities is still relatively new. Research is only now emerging regarding the strengths and limitations of this approach, but existing evidence seems to support access to the general curriculum as an approach that is capable of accomplishing the goals we noted previously (Downing, 2006; Smith, 2006; Wehmeyer, 2006). In addition, many efforts are underway to incorporate systematic instruction techniques, derived from applied behavior analysis, into opportunities to improve both access to the general curriculum *and* learning outcomes (Browder, Trela, & Jimenez, 2007; Copeland, Hughes, Agran, Wehmeyer, & Fowler, 2002; Jameson, McDonnell, Johnson, Riesen, & Polychronis, 2007).

Over the last several decades, emphasis on social relationships has grown and has increasingly become an area targeted in IEPs for students with disabilities. Because this book is focused on peer support interventions, which are based on the social interaction research literature, we provide a more in-depth treatment on social interaction in the section that follows.

Behind the Strategies

Trends in Educational Placement for Students with Severe Disabilities

Since the passage of the Education for All Handicapped Children Act (PL 94 142) in 1975, a gradual and steady shift has been apparent in the contexts within which students with severe disabilities receive educational services (Danielson & Bellamy, 1989; Katsiyannis, Zhang, & Archwamety, 2002). Whereas self-contained classrooms or separate schools once were the only option available to most students with severe disabilities, schools increasingly are shifting toward addressing the educational needs of these students within inclusive classrooms. Williamson, McLeskey, Hoppey, and Rentz (2006) analyzed educational placement trends throughout the 1990s and found that the proportion of students with intellectual disabilities who spent *some* to *most* of their school day in general education classrooms increased from 27% to 45%. A corresponding decrease in placement in self-contained classrooms and separate schools also was apparent. Williamson and colleagues, however, concluded that "where a student lives is often a stronger predictor of class placement than the nature or severity of the student's disability" (p. 358). Despite this considerable progress, there is still much work to do to ensure that students with disabilities have full access to the learning and social opportunities available within their schools. According to the *Twenty-Seventh Annual Report to Congress on the Implementation of the Individuals with Disabilities Education Act* (U.S. Department of Education, 2005), 6% of students with intellectual disabilities, 25% of students with multiple disabilities, and 12% of students with autism still receive their education in separate schools. In addition, placement patterns suggest that general education enrollment often becomes more restricted as students progress through middle and high school.

SOCIAL INTERACTION RESEARCH
FOR STUDENTS WITH SEVERE DISABILITIES

The first social interaction interventions for people with severe disabilities were developed for children receiving early childhood special education services (Odom, McConnell, & McEvoy, 1992). Prior to the extension to students with severe disabilities, Strain and Timm (1974) had demonstrated that social skills training techniques could be effective for students with behavior disorders. The work of Strain and Timm built on earlier uses of applied behavior analysis to establish social skills in socially isolated, typically developing children (Hart, Reynolds, Baer, Brawley, & Harris, 1968; Harris, Wolf, & Baer, 1964; Milby, 1970). Following on these early successes, a number of researchers began teaching social skills to children with severe disabilities to accelerate the development of emerging social repertoires and allow children to contact "new communities of reinforcement" that they might not otherwise be able to reach (Brady et al., 1985; Fox et al., 1984; Odom & Strain, 1986; Ragland, Kerr, & Strain, 1978).

The first application of social skills training for adolescents with severe disabilities occurred in the mid-1980s (Gaylord-Ross, Haring, Breen, & Pitts-Conway, 1984). Gaylord-Ross and colleagues adapted prompting and positive reinforcement techniques developed within early childhood settings, teaching high school students with autism how to reciprocally interact with their peers without disabilities. These findings were followed by a flurry of research over the next decade on teaching social skills to secondary age students with severe disabilities (Gaylord-Ross & Haring, 1987; Hughes, Harmer, Killian, & Niarhos, 1995; Hunt, Alwell, & Goetz, 1991; Sasso & Rude, 1987). These findings established that complex social interaction skills could be taught to youth with severe disabilities and that same-age peers without disabilities could both provide instruction and serve as conversational partners. However, one characteristic of this work, which was reflective of special education services at the time, was that it was typically conducted in special education classrooms and based on a curriculum that emphasized daily living skills.

In the early 1990s, following an influential policy paper published by then U.S. Department of Education Assistant Secretary Madeleine Will (1986), researchers and policy makers began focusing more prominently on the provision of special education services full time in general education environments, and the term *inclusion* began to be used to refer to this initiative. Within this policy context, Haring and Breen (1992) developed a peer-mediated intervention strategy that could be used outside of special education classrooms and was designed for the primary purpose of increasing social interactions. In addition, for the first time, research also focused on establishing friendships as an outcome of the social interaction intervention.

Extending the work of Haring and Breen (1992), Kennedy and Itkonen (1994) implemented peer-mediated interventions in general education classrooms and began to adopt techniques for curricular adaptations that were being proposed at the time (Calculator & Jorgensen, 1994; Falvey, 1995). It became apparent during this period that two issues were barriers to greater general education participation. First, many special education programs were adopting interventions for general education class participation, but peers were being overlooked as critical components of the intervention package. Instead, there was a growing reliance on paraprofessionals to support students in regular classes. This use of paraprofessionals had the unintended effect of isolating a student with severe disabilities from the other students in the classroom, thus limiting social interactions with peers without disabilities (Giangreco, Edelman, Broer, & Doyle, 2001).

The second barrier was curricular. In the early 1990s, curricular approaches for students with severe disabilities in K–12 environments still focused on daily living and other functional skills as an organizing theme for instructional content. This daily living skills orientation, however, did not mesh well with the curricular content being provided in general education environments. The result was that students with severe disabilities and students without disabilities were being taught two different curricula in the same classroom (Jorgensen, 1996; Stainback & Stainback, 1992). Thus, students were working on different materials, which removed a critical basis for commonality in the classroom. Combined with the concern about paraprofessionals being the primary source of instructional intervention, these two issues loomed as significant impediments to the policy goals set forward in inclusive education (Janney, Snell, Beers, & Raynes, 1995; Roach, Salisbury, & McGregor, 2002).

These converging concerns led researchers to develop approaches to instruction in general education classrooms that focused on access to the general education curriculum and systematic instruction delivered by peers without disabilities. In general, these strategies—now referred to as *peer support strategies*—represent an important step forward (Carter & Kennedy, 2006).

By focusing on the general curriculum, students with severe disabilities work within the same curricular framework as peers without disabilities, which emphasizes commonalities in what is learned and allows students to work together on the same materials. In addition, having peers without disabilities support involvement in class activities and provide systematic instruction promotes social interactions and fosters the development of social relationships. It also encourages paraprofessionals or other special educators to serve as resources for the whole general education classroom, providing additional assistance to the general educator.

The research on peer support strategies, to date, shows several promising outcomes that are improvements over the previous techniques used to facilitate social interactions. First, learning of academic content and acquisition of new skills is enhanced in peer support interventions, not only for students with severe disabilities but also for classmates without disabilities who serve as peer supports (Cushing & Kennedy, 1997; Dugan et al., 1995). Second, frequent and high-quality social interactions occur in these instructional contexts that can spill over into other settings in and out of school and can result in lasting friendships (Hunt, Soto, Maier, & Doering, 2003; Kamps, Barbetta, Leonard, & Delquadri, 1994; Kennedy, Shukla, & Fryxell, 1997). Finally, students with severe disabilities show increases in perceived classroom membership, which helps emphasize commonalities rather than differences among students (Salisbury, Gallucci, Palombaro, & Peck, 1995; Staub, Spaulding, Peck, Gallucci, & Schwartz, 1996). Indeed, in a relatively short time period, peer support interventions have received enough research scrutiny to be considered evidence-based practice by current policy standards (Horner et al., 2005).

By focusing on the general curriculum, students with severe disabilities work within the same curricular framework as peers without disabilities, which emphasizes commonalities in what is learned and allows students to work together on the same materials.

CONCLUSION

At this point, rather than move into an extended discussion of the elements of peer support interventions, which is covered in the next chapter, we would like to finish this chapter by saying a few words about these strategies. First, peer support interventions represent an evolution in practices for students with severe disabilities. As this chapter has outlined, this approach to intervention has clear antecedents—all of which have focused on improving the lives of students with severe disabilities and which have been adapted and improved on as educational practices and societal attitudes toward these students have changed. Thus, peer support interventions are representative of our current, best efforts as a field.

Second, peer support interventions should be used in conjunction with other evidence-based practices to provide a holistic and individualized support package for students with severe disabilities. Peer support interventions have evolved to target multiple outcomes, something that differentiates them from their predecessors. For example, academic and social outcomes can improve for students with and without disabilities who participate in peer support interventions. However, educational supports for students with severe disabilities need to encompass a larger set of contexts and outcomes than any single intervention can provide. This includes environments such as home, community, and the wider school campus (e.g., extracurricular clubs, student government); as well as a range of outcomes, including academic, social, daily living, communication, and behavioral improvements.

Finally, peer support interventions are different from many of the previous intervention approaches for students with severe disabilities, which have been based on one-to-one instructional interactions with an adult. Although one-to-one, adult-delivered interventions are very effective for teaching certain types of skills, social interactions and friendships by their nature require a different approach. Peer support arrangements necessarily incorporate classmates without disabilities as primary individuals in the intervention approach. In addition, it has become very clear that the best social interaction outcomes are achieved by students participating in inclusive school environments, rather than special education or segregated settings. Thus, to use peer support interventions, special educators need to develop and manage these intervention skills by partnering with others to achieve desired student outcomes. This element of adult and student collaboration is a key component in the effective use of peer support interventions but is a departure from the traditional ways that teachers often deliver educational programming.

2

The Practice and Promise of Peer Support Interventions

Ms. Martino was fairly adamant that her son Joseph should have a paraprofessional when he started seventh grade. Because Waubesa Middle School was fully inclusive, she was concerned the teachers in each of Joseph's seven different general education classes might not understand her son's specialized needs well enough to teach him, especially given how large most of these classes seemed to be. Ms. Martino also was worried that other students might not be very welcoming of Joseph, who had severe cognitive disabilities, and that he would need some help making friends. She felt that having a consistent adult assigned to work with Joseph across the school day would ensure that he got more out of class and made social connections with his classmates. His general education teachers welcomed the idea of having the paraprofessional and appreciated an extra set of hands in the classroom. And Joseph's special education teacher, already feeling a bit stretched with a fairly large caseload of students, agreed it was a good idea. A new paraprofessional was hired, and after attending the district's new employee orientation session, Ellen began working with Joseph across all of his classes. Ellen made sure Joseph went from one class to the next without ever being late and always had everything he needed for class. She sat next to him to help with assignments, answered all of his questions, and made sure he was always paying attention. As the semester progressed, the curriculum became more difficult, and Ellen began pulling Joseph aside more and more to work on alternative assignments. Trusting that Ellen knew more about meeting Joseph's specialized needs than they did, the classroom teachers tended to defer instructional responsibility to Ellen. Ellen did her best to modify class activities when she could, but she began to wonder whether Joseph really got anything out of being in these classes. Eventually the two began working on completely different activities that Ellen felt were more appropriate for Joseph. By the end of the semester, unfortunately, Joseph had learned very little of the general curriculum in his classes and knew few of his classmates.

Recent legislative and policy initiatives are raising expectations for students with severe disabilities by calling upon schools to ensure that *every* student has the services and supports he or she needs to access a challenging curriculum, participate in meaningful learning experiences, and enjoy valued relationships with peers. General education classrooms, extracurricular clubs, and other inclusive school activities have emerged as the preferred environments for meeting the educational and social needs of students with severe disabilities (Browder & Spooner, 2006; Kennedy & Horn, 2004). Although the proportion of the school day that students with disabilities are spending in these classrooms, clubs, and activities has increased since the early 1990s (Wagner, Cadwallader, & Marder, 2003; Williamson et al., 2006), educators and administrators continue to explore how best to support students with severe disabilities to participate fully and meaningfully in the general curriculum and life of their school.

SUPPORTING INCLUSION AND ACCESSING THE GENERAL CURRICULUM

Emergence of Paraprofessional Support

The prevailing approach used to support the general education participation of students with severe disabilities is the use of individually assigned paraprofessionals. Indeed, Suter and Giangreco (in press) noted that a visitor to most schools may increasingly expect to find more paraprofessionals than special educators working directly with students with disabilities. The U.S. Department of Education (2007) reported that more than 312,000 paraprofessionals (e.g., teaching assistants, instructional aides) provide special education and related services for children and youth with disabilities in the United States. Indeed, virtually every student with disabilities attends a school employing at least one paraprofessional (Wagner, Newman, Cameto, Levine, & Marder, 2003), and in many states the number of paraprofessionals exceeds the number of special educators.

The use of one-to-one paraprofessionals to support general education participation is especially pervasive for students with severe disabilities. What factors lead schools to turn to paraprofessionals as the primary avenue of support? A variety of reasons are often given for assigning one-to-one paraprofessionals to promote school inclusion (Giangreco, Yuan, McKenzie, Cameron, & Fialka, 2005; Suter & Giangreco, in press):

- Parents sometimes request one-to-one paraprofessionals during IEP meetings, believing 1) their children's instructional needs can be met only with intensive adult support, 2) their children will not be accepted by peers within the classroom without adult facilitation, and/or 3) general educators are not sufficiently prepared to teach their children effectively.

- General educators often request that a paraprofessional accompany students with extensive support needs who are included in their classroom, expressing concern about their own ability to teach an increasingly diverse class of students, to provide sufficient support to so many students without extra assistance, or to address substantial behavioral challenges.

- When large numbers of students are served, special educators often report difficulties finding time to be present in every classroom in which their students are included, to co-teach with general educators, and to provide direct instruction and support to students. Increasingly, special educators are assuming "case management" roles in which they supervise paraprofessionals who are providing direct support to students in inclusive classrooms.

- School districts may perceive paraprofessionals to be a less expensive option than hiring additional certified teachers.

Emerging Concerns

Like many educational trends, the rapid expansion of paraprofessionals has not been driven by research findings. In fact, the use of individually assigned paraprofessionals remains a service delivery approach currently lacking empirical support (Giangreco, Edelman, et al., 2001; Giangreco, Suter, & Doyle, in press). Although paraprofessionals can serve an important supplemental role in supporting students with disabilities (Causton-Theoharis & Malmgren, 2005b; Lane, Fletcher, Carter, Dejud, & Delorenzo, 2007), there is a glaring absence of research studies demonstrating that one-to-one paraprofessional supports are either necessary to promote curricular access or more effective than other approaches for supporting inclusion.

It is important to emphasize that the consequences of relying heavily on individually assigned paraprofessionals are also not neutral. Indeed, a number of unintended consequences have been documented widely in the research literature. Consider the following concerns raised about the overreliance on adult-delivered one-to-one support in inclusive classrooms:

- Students may have fewer interactions with their classmates when always accompanied by an adult, particularly during adolescence, when peer groups assume greater importance (Carter, Sisco, Brown, Brickham, & Al-Khabbaz, in press; Marks, Schrader, & Levine, 1999).
- Students may feel stigmatized by the constant presence of an adult at their side or isolated from their classmates when paraprofessionals implement instructional programming separate from the rest of the class (Broer, Doyle, & Giangreco, 2005; Giangreco et al., 2005).
- Students may have few interactions with certified, highly qualified teachers because instructional responsibility often is deferred to paraprofessionals (Giangreco, Broer, & Edelman, 2001).
- Student achievement and academic engagement may be hindered because paraprofessionals typically lack the training and supervision necessary to assume primary responsibility for instructional and curricular decision making (Gerber, Finn, Achilles, & Boyd-Zaharias, 2001; Malmgren & Causton-Theoharis, 2006).
- Students may develop unhealthy or inappropriate relationships with paraprofessionals, considering them to be among their primary friends or becoming overly dependent on their assistance (Broer et al., 2005; Giangreco & Broer, 2005).
- Students may receive fewer opportunities to develop skills promoting self-determination when everything is done for them or on their behalf (Giangreco et al., 2005).
- Students may be more likely to engage in challenging behavior when they have little voice in how they are supported or when paraprofessionals lack sufficient training in behavioral support strategies (Carter, O'Rourke, Sisco, & Pelsue, in press; Conroy, Asmus, Ladwig, Sellers, & Valcante, 2004).
- The assignment of one-to-one paraprofessionals may prevent students from actively determining their own need for support and the avenues by which that support will be provided (Giangreco et al., 2005).

Need for Alternative Support Models

Not surprisingly, these unintended drawbacks have led to renewed calls for schools to reduce their growing reliance on individually assigned adults to promote inclusion, access to the general curriculum, and peer relationships. At the same time, schools are being challenged to more closely scrutinize their service delivery models and to identify alternative approaches that contribute to better outcomes and greater school participation for students (Giangreco & Broer, 2007). However, responding to these calls requires a multifaceted approach addressing where students are served, how staff are trained, how planning is implemented, the ways teachers collaborate, how supports are allocated, and how evaluation is conducted. *Peer support arrangements* are emerging as one important component of this approach and have been identified as a recommended alternative to the extensive reliance on one-to-one, adult-delivered supports (Causton-Theoharis & Malmgren, 2005a; Downing, 2006; Giangreco, Halvorsen, Doyle, & Broer, 2004; Kleinert, Miracle, & Sheppard-Jones, 2007).

WHAT ARE PEER SUPPORT ARRANGEMENTS?

Peer support arrangements are a promising approach for promoting access to rigorous, relevant learning experiences; expanding opportunities for students to establish new relationships with their peers; and helping educators and paraprofessionals to support inclusive education more effectively. Put simply, these intervention strategies involve arranging *for one or more peers without disabilities to provide ongoing social and academic support to their classmates with severe disabilities while receiving guidance and support from paraprofessionals, special educators, and/or general educators* (Carter, Cushing, & Kennedy, 2008; Carter & Kennedy, 2006; Cushing & Kennedy, 1997). Recognizing that peers are an underutilized—but widely available—source of natural support in every school, peer support arrangements draw upon the involvement of other classmates to assist in helping students with disabilities participate more fully in the social and learning opportunities existing in inclusive classrooms, extracurricular clubs, and other school activities.

   Peer-mediated approaches—in which students assume instructional or other support roles with their classmates—have been a staple intervention strategy in classrooms for as long as there have been schools (Harper & Maheady, 2007). Indeed, countless variations on these approaches exist—ranging from informal, casual pairings of students to more structured, intentional systems (Gillies, 2007). As these strategies have been tested in the classroom and refined through research, a powerful and effective set of techniques have emerged for use with students with disabilities (e.g., Goldstein, Schneider, & Thiemann, 2007; Heron, Villareal, Ma, Christianson, & Heron, 2006; Maheady, Harper, & Mallette, 2001). Although peer support arrangements share the strong theoretical and empirical support

Peer support arrangements involve arranging for one or more peers without disabilities to provide ongoing social and academic support to their classmates with severe disabilities while receiving guidance and support.

of other peer-mediated strategies, they also differ in important ways. First, in peer support arrangements, somewhat greater emphasis typically is placed on exchanging social support, encouraging peer interactions, and promoting social connections. Social goals are often prominent in the IEPs of students with severe disabilities, and general education participation frequently is advocated for as an avenue for meeting these goals. Second, unlike other peer-mediated interventions in which all participating students assume very structured or static roles (e.g.,

Classwide Peer Tutoring [Greenwood, Arreaga-Mayer, Utley, Gavin, & Terry, 2001], Peer Assisted Learning Strategies [McMaster, Fuchs, & Fuchs, 2006]), educators are encouraged to individually tailor peer support interventions so that they reflect the unique support needs, strengths, and characteristics of participating students with disabilities and their peers. Third, peer support arrangements usually are not implemented as classwide interventions and thus involve a smaller number of peers. Fourth, most peer-mediated interventions were developed primarily for students with high-incidence disabilities such as learning disabilities or emotional or behavior disorders (Gardner, Nobel, Hessler, Yawn, & Heron,

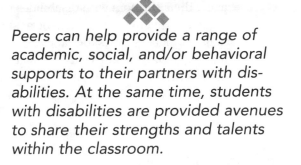

Peers can help provide a range of academic, social, and/or behavioral supports to their partners with disabilities. At the same time, students with disabilities are provided avenues to share their strengths and talents within the classroom.

2007). Recognizing that the academic and social support needs of students with severe disabilities may be more intensive, peer support arrangements typically offer a more sustained and focused source of support. Finally, peer support interventions are designed to be implemented in inclusive contexts. Self-contained classrooms or segregated school activities simply do not offer the same depth of natural support available in inclusive environments.

Core Components

Because peer support interventions should be individually tailored to address the instructional and social needs of students with disabilities, they can be implemented in a variety of ways. However, the following steps usually are taken when establishing these arrangements in inclusive classrooms:

- Identifying students with severe disabilities who need assistance to participate in class activities
- Recruiting peers from within the same classroom to help provide some of these supports
- Arranging for students to sit next to each other and remain in close proximity during class activities
- Orienting peers to their roles, explaining the rationale for their involvement, and showing them basic strategies for supporting the academic and social participation of their classmate
- Providing ongoing monitoring, feedback, and assistance to peers and their partners throughout the semester, as needed
- Shifting paraprofessionals to a broader support role in which they assist all students in the classroom or complete other responsibilities as directed by the teacher

How Students Work Together

Peers can help provide a range of academic, social, and/or behavioral supports to their partners with disabilities. For example, students might support the class participation of their partners by working together on assignments, sharing materials, encouraging involvement in cooperative groups, paraphrasing lectures, asking clarifying questions, reviewing work, offering constructive feedback, making sure that needed materials are available, or explaining how to complete part of an assignment. Peers can promote attainment of social-related educational goals by encouraging their partners with disabilities to interact socially, extending conversational turns, modeling contextually appropriate social skills, reinforcing communication attempts, and redirecting inappropriate conversational topics. They also encourage interactions with other classmates by making initial introductions, highlighting shared interests and other commonalities, and extending interactions outside of the classroom (e.g., lunch, extracurricular clubs, after-school activities). At the same time, students with disabilities are provided avenues to share their strengths and talents within the classroom.

Shifting Adult Roles

Peer support arrangements do not eliminate the need for individualized support but instead encourage paraprofessionals to assume different roles within inclusive classrooms. Paraprofessionals and other educators continue to take overall responsibility for ensuring that the educational needs of students with severe disabilities are being met, but they begin fading their direct support as students with disabilities and their peer partners become more comfortable working together. In other words, the roles of paraprofessionals and special educators broaden within inclusive classrooms, allowing them to provide assistance to, and work with, a wider range of students in the class. However, paraprofessionals continue to seek out ways to foster learning and interaction opportunities for the student with disabilities and always remain available to provide needed feedback and assistance to peers and their partners. Moreover, paraprofessionals assume responsibilities that generally are not appropriate for peers, such as responding to substantial behavioral challenges, addressing medical or personal care needs, documenting IEP progress and learning, and adapting assignments (under the supervision of the special educator).

A Flexible Intervention Strategy

Although the above-mentioned core elements—selecting students, orienting peers, pairing students, and adult monitoring—represent the basic ingredients of peer support interventions, these strategies can be implemented flexibly in a variety of ways. Research suggests that peer support interventions represent a fairly robust approach to improving social and academic participation 1) across the grade span; 2) within a wide variety of school environments; and 3) when combined or embedded with other tactics, instructional arrangements, and support strategies.

Across the Grade Span

The educational and social landscape clearly changes as students progress through elementary, middle, and high school. *Academically*, differences across the school levels are evidenced in the focus and complexity of the curriculum, the primary approaches teachers use to provide instruction, the avenues through which students work together, and teachers' expectations for students' performance. *Socially*, the importance of peers in the lives of children broadens over time, the nature of their relationships evolves, the contexts in which students spend time expand, and the skills needed to successfully navigate peer relations change (Goldstein & Morgan, 2002). *Behaviorally*, teachers' beliefs about what constitutes appropriate behavior varies, their expectations for students' independence and self-determination changes, and different risk factors emerge as more salient influences on children's development (Lane, Pierson, Stang, & Carter, in press). And *structurally*, primary and secondary schools differ substantively in size, teacher–student ratios, team models, staffing patterns, and organization.

Peer support arrangements can readily be tailored to reflect these contextual differences. Indeed, research documenting the effectiveness of peer support arrangements has been implemented from early elementary through high school. In elementary school, inclusion in general education typically is more common, students spend most of their day with the same peers, the presence of adults typically is not a hindrance to peer interaction, and teachers tend to rely more heavily on cooperative learning activities. Peer support arrangements with younger students often involve rotating peers, explicitly targeting especially social times of the school day (e.g., recess, playgroups, station time), and may require more active adult facilitation (Dugan et al., 1995; Laushey & Heflin, 2000; Salisbury et al., 1995). During the middle grades, students begin rotating classrooms, peer affiliations become more important, and students are given greater independence. Peer support interventions drawing upon peer networks appear to be particularly promising for these early adolescents (Garrison-Harrell, Kamps, & Kravitz, 1997; Kamps, Dugan, Potucek, & Collins, 1999). In high school, the emphasis on academic support often becomes more prominent within peer support arrangements and efforts to promote relationships that spill over outside of the classroom usually have to be more deliberate (e.g., Carter, Sisco, Melekoglu, & Kurkowski, in press; Haring & Breen, 1992). It is this flexibility to address the needs of students across the grade span that makes peer support interventions an especially appealing strategy for educators.

Across School Environments

Although increasing participation in core academic classes such as language arts, math, science, and social studies is central to recent school reform efforts, the general education curriculum also can be thought of more broadly as the full spectrum of social and learning experiences available to students within a school (Ryndak & Billingsley, 2004). Peer support strategies can be implemented across a wide range of school contexts, including the following:

- Academic, elective, vocational, and related arts classrooms (Carter & Kennedy, 2006; Shukla, Kennedy, & Cushing, 1998, 1999)
- Service-learning projects (Dymond, Renzaglia, & Chun, 2007; Kleinert et al., 2004)
- Extracurricular clubs (Kleinert et al., 2007)
- Community-based activities (Vandercook, 1991)
- Lunchrooms (Kamps, Lopez, & Golden, 2002; Miller, Cooke, Test, & White, 2003)
- Between classes and before and after school (Gaylord-Ross et al., 1984; Haring & Breen, 1992)

Of course, the roles that peers and their partners with disabilities assume, as well as the ways in which they work and interact together, may look somewhat different across each of these environments and activities.

Combining Strategies

Peer support strategies also can—and often should—be combined with other intervention approaches into more comprehensive support packages. For example, teachers who frequently use cooperative learning within their classrooms may still embed peer support strategies within these groupings. Cushing, Kennedy, Shukla, Davis, and Meyer (1997) offered one example of how peer support arrangements could be woven into cooperative learning groups for two students with severe disabilities enrolled in an eighth-grade English class. Although all students with and without disabilities assumed different roles within these cooperative groups (i.e., organizer, materials manager, checker, recorder), one student in each group volunteered to provide more intentional support by helping promote communication and curricular access for each student with disabilities. Similarly, Gilberts, Agran, Hughes, and Wehmeyer (2001) demonstrated how peer support strategies could be combined with student-directed learning strategies to help five middle school students with severe disabilities participate more actively and independently in Spanish, history, art, and reading classes. Such hybrid interventions demonstrate how educators can tailor these peer support arrangements to promote student participation within their classroom, but to do so in ways that fit well with typical classroom routines.

Research indicates that peer support interventions offer an effective approach for improving social outcomes for both students with and without disabilities.

RESEARCH ON SOCIAL AND ACADEMIC BENEFITS

A substantial body of research has addressed the roles peers can play in promoting the social and academic participation of their classmates with disabilities (see Bellini, Peters, Brianner, & Hopf, 2007; Carter & Hughes, 2005; Carter & Kennedy, 2006; Goldstein, Kaczmarek, & English, 2002; McConnell, 2002). Collectively, findings from these studies are challenging the widespread—and often exclusive use—of paraprofessionals to support school inclusion and suggest students with severe disabilities may actually have more interactions with their classmates and be more academically engaged when receiving support from their peers. In the following sections, we review this research in greater detail and describe some of the factors that may contribute to the effectiveness of peer support strategies.

Peer Interactions and Social Relationships

Peer relationships can make important contributions to students' development, influence their engagement in school, and impact their well-being and overall quality of life. Yet, middle and high school can be a particularly vulnerable time socially for students with severe disabilities. As students move through secondary school, general education involvement often becomes more limited and friendships more elusive for students with disabilities (Carter, Hughes, Guth, & Copeland, 2005; Orsmond, Krauss, & Seltzer, 2004; U.S. Department of Education, 2005). Among students receiving special education services, youth with autism, multiple disabilities, deaf-blindness, and intellectual disabilities are the least likely students to have active friendships during high school (Wagner, Newman, et al., 2003). Such social isolation can place students at elevated risk for negative social outcomes that could continue into adulthood (McIntyre, Kraemer, Blacher, & Simmerman, 2004; Sandstrom & Zakriski, 2004).

Reversing these outcomes starts by making sure that students with and without disabilities have meaningful opportunities to meet, spend time together, and develop friendships with each other. But, it takes much more than increased proximity to ensure that students actually interact with and get to know each other (see Behind the Strategies on this page). Students' attitudes about their classmates with severe disabilities do not necessarily change simply because they are attending the same school or are enrolled in the same classes (Siperstein, Norins, & Mohler, 2007). Thoughtful, well-planned, and intentional efforts are essential to fostering relationships. Research indicates that peer support interventions offer just such an effective approach for improving social outcomes for both students with and without disabilities.

Benefits for Students with Disabilities

A plethora of studies have documented how students with disabilities benefit socially when they receive support from their peers. For example, Shukla and colleagues (1998, 1999) examined the social benefits associated with peer support arrangements for middle school students enrolled in core academic (e.g., English, math, social studies) and elective (e.g., industrial arts, music, art) classrooms. Students with severe disabilities interacted more frequently with classmates

---

Behind the Strategies

It Takes More Than Simply Being in the Same Place

Although increasing access to the general curriculum has emerged as a central theme of recent standards-based reform efforts, enrolling students in general education classrooms is only the first step toward ensuring that students reap the myriad social and academic benefits available within inclusive classrooms. Observational research consistently confirms that without carefully designed support strategies and intentional planning, students with severe disabilities are unlikely to interact frequently with their classmates or participate fully in ongoing instruction (e.g., Carter, Hughes, Guth, & Copeland, 2005; Dymond & Russell, 2004). For example, Carter, Sisco, Brown, Brickham, and Al-Khabbaz (in press) spent more than 150 hours observing in middle and high school classrooms that included youth with intellectual disabilities and autism. Despite attending the same class as their peers in natural proportions, these students with disabilities had few conversations with their classmates and experienced limited access to the general curriculum. Indeed, students with disabilities did not interact with another classmate during almost one-quarter of all classroom observations. Similarly, Wehmeyer, Lattin, Lapp-Rincker, and Agran (2003) spent more than 100 hours in a range of middle school classrooms observing how 33 students with intellectual disabilities accessed the general curriculum. Students with severe disabilities were actively engaged in learning tasks aligned to district standards only 55% of the time. Unless educators and paraprofessionals take an active role in promoting social and learning opportunities for students, the many potential benefits available within inclusive classrooms will remain elusive.

and accessed a greater variety of social supports—such as information, material aid, emotional support, and companionship—when working with a peer, compared with working exclusively with a paraprofessional. Similarly, Carter, Hughes, and colleagues (2005) found that high school students with disabilities had more frequent, higher quality interactions when working with a peer across a range of school environments. Moreover, students' interactions with the peers with whom they were partnered tend to be fairly reciprocal and balanced across both academic and social topics, easing concerns that such arrangements necessarily encourage primarily tutorial or hierarchical relationships (Carter, Sisco, Melekoglu, & Kurkowski, in press). In other words, students with disabilities are not socially passive in these arrangements, always at the receiving end of a stream of instructions, directives, and questions. When teachers rely heavily on lecture and independent seatwork—particularly in middle and high school—peer support arrangements appear to create opportunities for promoting interaction, building social skills, and fostering relationships that are often overlooked or otherwise unavailable in these environments.

These social benefits are not just limited to increased social interactions (see Table 2.1). Students are likely to benefit in other ways when they have the opportunity to work with and get to know their peers. They may learn new social and communication skills (Hunt, Alwell, Farron-Davis, & Goetz, 1996; Weiner, 2005), meet more of their classmates (Kennedy & Itkonen, 1994; Kennedy, Shukla, & Fryxell, 1997), develop new friendships (Haring & Breen, 1992; Kennedy, Cushing, & Itkonen, 1997), access valued social supports (Meyer, 2001), attain important educational goals (Hunt, Staub, Alwell, & Goetz, 1994), and experience a greater sense of belonging and class membership (Schnorr, 1997).

Benefits for Peers

Peers also benefit socially when they work together with their classmates with disabilities (see Table 2.2). Through working with their partners, peers expand their own social networks, learn valuable social and support skills, and develop new friendships. Students who are given the opportunity to interact with their classmates with severe disabilities consistently speak of other important benefits, including personal growth, greater understanding of self, improved attitudes

Table 2.1.   How might students with severe disabilities benefit from working with their peers?

More frequent, higher quality interactions with classmates
Increased opportunities to receive *and* provide social support
Development of new friendships and supportive relationships
Expanded social networks
Increased class membership and sense of belonging
Broader participation in class and school activities
Increased social competence and improved social skills
Higher expectations from teachers and peers
Greater proficiency in the use of communication systems
Increased independence and self-determination
Acquisition of new academic and collateral skills
Greater academic engagement and curricular access
Progress toward educational goals
Access to a broader range of school activities
Receipt of less stigmatizing and intrusive sources of supports

Table 2.2. How might peers benefit from working with their class-mates with severe disabilities?

Greater academic engagement and class participation
Increased opportunities to receive *and* provide social support
Improved grades and homework completion
Acquisition of new support and advocacy skills
Additional attention and feedback from adults
Lasting friendships
Sense of accomplishment and personal growth
Appreciation for the importance and value of inclusion
Increased self-confidence and assumption of greater responsibility
Greater appreciation of diversity and individual differences
Deeper knowledge about and understanding of specific disabilities
Improved attitudes toward people with disabilities
Increased class and school attendance

toward people with disabilities, greater appreciation of diversity, new advocacy skills, and lasting friendships (e.g., Carter, Hughes, Copeland, & Breen, 2001; Copeland et al., 2004; Hughes et al., 2001; Kamps et al., 1998; Kishi & Meyer, 1994). Indeed, the reciprocal nature of these benefits highlights the value of these intervention strategies for all students.

Why Do These Strategies Work?

What makes peer support arrangements such a promising avenue for promoting interactions and friendships among students with and without disabilities? When it comes to peer relationships, context definitely matters (Gifford-Smith & Brownell, 2003). Peer support arrangements create a context within which interactions among students are encouraged, facilitated, and supported, addressing many of the common barriers to accessing the peer social environment often existing in classrooms and other school environments (see Behind the Strategies on p. 19). Consider the following factors that can limit opportunities for peer interaction.

- *Limited proximity:* Students cannot converse and work with each other if they are not in close proximity. It is all too common to observe students with severe disabilities working with a paraprofessional on the peripheries of the classroom or even pulled aside to other locations for more individualized instruction. Peer support arrangements ensure that students are sitting among their classmates and are actively involved in shared activities.

- *Adult presence:* When a paraprofessional or special educator is always present, other students may be reluctant to or even discouraged from interacting directly with their classmate with disabilities (Han & Chadsey, 2004; Meyer, 2001). Peers are implicitly taught that their interactions have to be channeled through an adult. Although most classmates naturally turn to each other for assistance with class activities and assignments, students with disabilities often look to their paraprofessional for help with their classwork rather than asking their peers for assistance; similarly, other students may assume it is the paraprofessional's responsibility to help. During adolescence, the growing influence of peers and the potential stigma associated with always "hanging out" with adults can also hinder interactions. Middle and high school students typically prefer not to have conversations about their peers, popular culture, upcoming social events, after-school activities, and other topics when adults are always within earshot.

- *Peer perceptions:* Students' perceptions of the capabilities of students with disabilities can have a strong influence on their willingness to interact with these classmates during the school day (Siperstein, Parker, Bardon, & Widaman, 2007). When students with severe disabilities are always anchored to an adult, it further reinforces classmates' perceptions of difference and communicates that students may have little to contribute to the class. When peers instead see students with disabilities working together with their classmates on common learning activities, they may see their classmates as more competent and recognize more of what they share in common. This may increase the likelihood that these peers will initiate interactions.

- *Instructional approaches:* When teachers rely heavily on lectures and independent seatwork—instructional formats that are widespread within many middle and high school classrooms and can limit interaction opportunities—peer support arrangements create teacher-approved avenues for students to still interact with each other. For example, students may share materials, work jointly on assignments, or review one another's work. As students work together, more initiations are directed to students with disabilities and peers are more likely to reinforce students' interaction attempts.

- *Initial uncertainty:* The initial information and strategies shared with students—coupled with ongoing feedback and support provided by paraprofessionals and educators—helps ensure peers feel comfortable and confident when interacting with their partners with disabilities (Copeland et al., 2004; Downing, 2005a). These orientation activities can help overcome any initial uncertainty or hesitation students might have about how to interact with someone who engages in stereotypical behavior, uses an augmentative communication device, or communicates in unconventional ways.

- *Skill deficits:* Most students with severe disabilities experience substantial challenges in the areas of language, communication, or social interaction skills. When working with their peers, students gain additional opportunities to practice and refine these skills, observe them being modeled by peers, and receive feedback from others on the appropriateness of their social behaviors. As the real experts on those social skills considered acceptable and likely to be reinforced at the school, peers may actually be more effective at encouraging and promoting appropriate conversational and social skills than adults, especially during adolescence (Prater, Bruhl, & Serna, 1998).

- *Peer networks:* Students have an understanding of the peer culture and a perspective on social relationships that adults generally are not privy to. They know who hangs out with whom and can help students with disabilities connect with peer groups in ways adults cannot. Moreover, peers introduce their partners to their own friendship networks, facilitating interactions with a much broader range of students within and beyond the classroom.

Academic Engagement and Learning Outcomes

Although the social benefits associated with general education participation have long been advocated as a principal rationale for inclusion (Brown, Branston, Hamre-Nietupski, Johnson, et al., 1979), schools also are recognizing the importance of raising expectations for what students with severe disabilities can and should learn. As addressed in Chapter 1, educators must now ensure students access rigorous and relevant learning opportunities within the general curriculum. Responding meaningfully to this call continues to challenge educators, especially at the

Behind the Strategies

What Do Peers Say About Fostering Friendships in School?

When asked what barriers to social relationships among students with and without severe disabilities exist in their schools, educators often point to the attitudes and willingness of other classmates. The research literature suggests, however, that peers may be quite willing to play a role in supporting the academic and social participation of their classmates with severe disabilities (Fisher, 1999; Peck, Donaldson, & Pezzoli, 1990; York & Tundidor, 1995). In their examination of the friendship expectations of middle school students toward their peers with severe disabilities, Han and Chadsey (2004) found it was not negative attitudes of classmates that peers raised as the principle barrier to friendships but rather the limited opportunities students were given to get to know each other. Indeed, the three most common reasons students gave for not having friendships with their peers with severe disabilities were 1) they were not enrolled in the same classes, 2) they had few opportunities to see each other in school, and 3) paraprofessionals were always present. Copeland and colleagues (2004) held focus group interviews with 53 high school students who had served as peer supports for at least one semester. These students also noted that limited general education and extracurricular participation decreased the opportunities that existed for students with severe disabilities to participate academically and socially in the life of their school. Yet, the students who were interviewed recognized their own role in promoting interaction opportunities, modeling acceptance, and advocating for their classmates with severe disabilities. Finally, in their survey of more than 1,100 middle school students, Hendrickson, Shokoohi-Yekta, Hamre-Nietupski, and Gable (1996) found that students thought it was important for them to develop friendships with their peers with disabilities and recognized their own role in facilitating these relationships.

middle and high school level. It is during these grades that the curriculum becomes more demanding, instruction tends to move at a faster pace, teachers rely less on cooperative and small-group learning, expectations for independent student performance increase, and the "performance" gap between students with and without severe disabilities widens.

For meaningful inclusion to occur within general education classrooms, educators must be very intentional about planning instructional and support strategies that more fully engage youth in learning opportunities. Simply being present in classrooms where the general curriculum is delivered does not automatically ensure that students will be active participants in the same learning opportunities as their classmates (Lee, Soukup, Little, & Wehmeyer, in press; Wehmeyer, Lattin, Lapp-Rincker, & Agran, 2003). In their observations of middle and high school classrooms, Carter, Sisco, Brown, and colleagues (in press) found that students with intellectual disabilities or autism were engaged less than 60% of the time in learning activities aligned with those delivered to the class as a whole. Since the late 1990s, a growing number of effective strategies for promoting meaningful engagement in a range of academic, elective, related arts, and vocational classrooms have been identified in the research literature (e.g., Browder & Spooner, 2006; Lee et al., 2006; Spooner et al., 2006). Research suggests that peer support interventions may be a particularly effective approach for improving academic outcomes for both students with *and* without severe disabilities.

Benefits for Students with Disabilities

Peer support arrangements may promote engagement in instructional activities at least as well as, if not better than, one-to-one paraprofessional supports. For example, Shukla and colleagues (1998, 1999) demonstrated that middle school students with severe disabilities were more engaged in ongoing class activities and had greater access to instructional content aligned with the general curriculum when they received primary support from a peer. For the remaining students, academic engagement did not differ depending on whether peers or adults provided direct support. Carter, Cushing, Clark, and Kennedy (2005) showed that middle and high school students with severe disabilities maintained high levels of academic engagement when they worked with one or two peers in inclusive science and English classes.

The research literature contains numerous demonstrations of how peer-delivered instruction can promote learning, academic engagement, and skill acquisition for students with moderate to severe disabilities. For example, peers have effectively assisted their classmates in learning a wide variety of academic and life skills, including

- Spelling (Browder & Xin, 1998; Miracle, Collins, Schuster, & Grisham-Brown, 2001)
- Reading (Collins, Branson, & Hall, 1995)
- Letter writing (Collins, Branson, Hall, & Rankin, 2001)
- Math (Butler, Miller, Lee, & Pierce, 2001; McDonnell, Mathot-Buckner, Thorson, & Fister, 2001; Schloss & Kobza, 1997)
- History (McDonnell et al., 2001)
- First aid (Marchand-Martella & Martella, 1992)
- Food preparation (Agran, Fodor-Davis, Moore, & Martella, 1992)
- Physical education (Halle, Gabler-Halle, & Chung, 1999; Ward & Ayvazo, 2006)
- Science (Carter, Sisco, Melekoglu, & Kurkowski, in press)

Benefits for Peers

Consistent with other peer-mediated interventions (e.g., Mastropieri, Scruggs, & Berkeley, 2007; Stenhoff & Lignugaris, 2007), research suggests that peer support strategies also provide important academic benefits to participating students without disabilities. Although administrators, parents, or teachers occasionally voice concerns about whether students may fall behind academically if expected to provide assistance to others, research suggests the opposite may be more likely to occur. Cushing and Kennedy (1997) tracked the academic engagement of three middle school students as each supported a classmate with moderate to severe disabilities in English, science, and health classes. These students—who were themselves struggling academically—all substantially increased their engagement in ongoing instruction, homework assignment completion, and classroom participation. Shukla and colleagues (1998, 1999) replicated these findings, demonstrating that peers either maintained or improved their levels of academic engagement when they worked with a

Peer support arrangements may promote engagement in instructional activities at least as well as, if not better than, one-to-one paraprofessional supports.

classmate with severe disabilities. This pattern of academic benefits for peers appears to be consistent across elementary school (Bensted & Bachor, 2002), middle school (McDonnell et al., 2001), and high school (Carter, Cushing, et al., 2005). Perhaps most compelling, however, is that these intervention strategies have proven especially effective for students who are at-risk for school failure. Such students often show improvements of one to two letter grades over the course of a semester when serving as a peer support (Kennedy, 2002b).

Why Do These Strategies Work?

Several factors may contribute to the effectiveness of peer support strategies at improving the academic outcomes and learning experiences of students with severe disabilities. Working with one or more peers can provide students with disabilities with individualized assistance, additional opportunities to respond, and more immediate feedback and reinforcement (Maheady et al., 2001). Peers help their partners participate in class activities, prompt them to stay on task, and provide needed assistance. Although paraprofessionals can certainly provide similar types of academic support, students with disabilities may be much more motivated to put forth effort when working alongside their peers (Gilberts et al., 2001). Peer support interventions also increase the number of people in the classroom who are watching to make sure that the curriculum is appropriately adapted, needed materials are available, and ongoing activities match those of other students in the classroom. In other words, peers are quick to point out when their partners are doing work that does not resemble their own, and they can be extremely creative at brainstorming ways to adjust activities so that everyone can participate. When peers learn basic instructional and support strategies as part of initial orientation activities, these students can be quite adept at helping their partners stay engaged and acquire new skills.

For peers without disabilities, the additional contact they have with adults in the classroom may underlie some of their academic improvements (Shukla et al., 1998). Paraprofessionals regularly monitor students as they work together, providing any feedback and assistance students may need, as well as troubleshooting any problems that arise. As a result, peers usually receive more individualized attention, academic help, and praise from adults in the classroom than they might otherwise receive when working independently. Peers also benefit personally from the support strategies they learn during initial orientation activities. They discover they learn more themselves when they know they are partially responsible for conveying or reinforcing key concepts and skills with their partner. To be effective in their support roles, peers have to make sure they pay close attention to lectures, understand the instructions of teachers, and know exactly what is expected of them. Finally, the relationships peers develop with their partners and adults in the classroom can have a motivating influence. When students develop new friendships and assume important responsibilities within the classroom, they may be more likely to want to attend class regularly. For some at-risk students, this also may be the only context in which they receive positive feedback and encouragement from adults.

Summary of Social and Academic Benefits

Collectively, this line of research is challenging the widespread perception that paraprofessionals are the preferred approach for supporting inclusion in school. The social and academic benefits of peer support arrangements are certainly promising for educators responsible for meeting the diverse educational needs of students with and without severe disabilities. Indeed, students' social and academic outcomes may be closely linked, as peer interactions both promote and provide the context for skill acquisition and content mastery (Hunt & McDonnell, 2007). These research findings should prompt educators to think much more deliberately about the approaches used to support the inclusion of students with severe disabilities in general education classes and other school activities.

SOCIAL VALIDITY AND CLASSROOM FIT

Clearly, it is important that educators have access to support strategies that work *and* are practical to use in their classrooms. Unfortunately, educators and administrators have long lamented what they perceive as a substantial disconnect between intervention strategies evaluated in the research literature and those considered to be feasible to implement in their classrooms and schools (Greenwood & Abbott, 2001; Snell, 2003). When an intervention simply does not fit well with current classroom practices, competes with other instructional priorities for time or resources, or is simply too difficult to use, it is unlikely to be adopted by educators regardless of its effectiveness (Boardman, Argüelles, Vaughn, Hughes, & Klingner, 2005). Peer support strategies not only have strong research backing—but just as importantly—they appear to be highly valued by teachers and students.

Paraprofessionals

Paraprofessionals frequently share that they are uncertain about the responsibilities they should and should not assume within inclusive classrooms and that they feel they receive little guidance on how best to support students with severe disabilities (Patterson, 2006; Wallace, 2003). Peer support interventions outline clear roles for paraprofessionals within these classrooms, clarifying the kinds of support and assistance they should provide to students with and without disabilities enrolled in a particular class. As their role within the classroom broadens, paraprofessionals often say they enjoy having the chance to get to know and work with a wider range of students. In their survey of high school staff, Carter and Pesko (2008) found that paraprofessionals who worked directly with students with severe disabilities perceived peer support strategies to be both effective and feasible to implement in general education classrooms. Moreover, paraprofessionals working across the grade span generally report feeling adequately prepared to supervise peer support arrangements in their schools (Carter, O'Rourke, et al., in press).

High school educators reported that peer support interventions enabled them to differentiate instruction more readily and to better meet the needs of all of their students.

Educators

A consistent theme in conversations with general and special educators surrounds their expressed need for practical strategies to include students with severe disabilities socially and academically in inclusive classrooms (Agran, Alper, & Wehmeyer, 2002; Carter & Hughes, 2006; Downing, Ryndak, & Clark, 2000). Peer support arrangements provide teachers with a flexible approach for addressing individualized support needs within increasingly diverse classrooms. When asked to share their experiences working with a schoolwide peer support program, high school general and special educators reported that peer support interventions enabled them to differentiate instruction more readily and to better meet the needs of all of their students (Copeland, McCall, et al., 2002). Moreover, general educators can typically establish peer support arrangements for students without having to restructure instructional practices for the entire class. Educators also frequently acknowledge that these interventions offer substantive benefits to *both* students with and without disabilities. Therefore, it is not surprising that peer support interventions such as these have garnered such widespread support among teachers across the grade span (Carter & Pesko, 2008; Odom, McConnell, & Chandler, 1994; Wagner, Newman, et al., 2003).

Administrators

Administrator support plays an influential role in determining whether or not an educational practice becomes a permanent part of a school's culture. The academic benefits associated with peer support interventions may be particularly appealing for administrators, especially in light of recent accountability mandates. At the same time, the benefits associated with personal growth, character development, and peer relationships for students also are likely to be valued (Jones, 2007). Although administrators are likely to wonder about the professional development and training staff might require in order to implement these strategies effectively, the ease with which educators and paraprofessionals can incorporate these strategies into their classrooms should allay such concerns.

Students with and without Disabilities

It is essential to consider the perspectives of students with and without disabilities, as they are the primary participants in and beneficiaries of peer support arrangements. A number of studies indicate that students without disabilities may recognize the important role they might play in supporting the inclusion, school involvement, and social relationships of their classmates with disabilities (Fisher, 1999; Hendrickson, Shokoohi-Yekta, Hamre-Nietupski, & Gable, 1996). As mentioned previously, students often speak vividly about the ways in which they feel they have personally benefited from their involvement in peer support programs. Themes from these conversations include learning more about people with disabilities, developing more positive attitudes, feeling a sense of accomplishment, gaining a greater appreciation of diversity, developing new friendships, learning new advocacy and support skills, increased empathy, and having higher expectations for their classmates (Copeland et al., 2004; Hughes et al., 2001; Jones, 2007; Kamps et al., 1998; Longwill & Kleinert, 1998; Whitaker, Barratt, Joy, Potter, & Thomas, 1998). Students with severe disabilities also may prefer learning alongside their peers rather than working with individually assigned adults. Interviews conducted with youth with severe disabilities highlighted a variety of concerns associated with receiving extensive paraprofessional support (Broer et al., 2005; Hemmingsson, Borell, & Gustavsson, 2003; Skär & Tamm, 2001). Actively involving students with disabilities in determining how and where they will be supported, as well as who will provide the support, is an essential step in designing peer support strategies that students will value highly.

WHAT PEER SUPPORT STRATEGIES ARE NOT

We have devoted the majority of this chapter to providing an overview of peer support interventions and their potential benefits. Peer support strategies certainly offer a promising avenue for promoting social relationships and access to the general curriculum for students with severe disabilities. However, it is important to acknowledge some limits of peer support interventions, so we close this chapter with a few caveats related to what peer support strategies are not.

- *Peer support interventions are not sufficient by themselves to sustain inclusion.* Peer support arrangements represent just one component of comprehensive educational programming for students. The numerous benefits highlighted in this chapter will always remain elusive if peer support arrangements are implemented apart from careful planning, collaborative teaming, relevant curricula, thoughtful adaptations, and effective instruction. Peer support arrangements should augment good instruction, not be implemented in lieu of it. They should be combined with other individualized support strategies—such as curricular and instructional modifications, related services, and other classroom-level practices— rather than be established in isolation.

- *Peers support interventions are not intended to eliminate the need for adult support.* The effectiveness of peer support arrangements does not imply that adult support is no longer needed or that paraprofessionals always hinder peer interaction and learning. Peer support arrangements ask educators to reconsider the roles of paraprofessionals within inclusive classrooms. Rather than serving as the exclusive source of support to students with severe disabilities, paraprofessionals should shift to more supplemental roles, providing direct support only when more natural supports are unavailable, insufficient, or cannot be accessed.

- *Peer support interventions are not automatic.* It takes more than simply seating two or more students next to each other to produce the academic and social outcomes described in this chapter. Peer support strategies work best when accompanied by thoughtful planning, ongoing adult guidance, and frequent monitoring. Like any individually designed supports, some massaging and refining may be required until the fit is just right.

CONCLUSION

Educators increasingly are being called upon to use evidence-based practices to promote improved outcomes for students with disabilities. The strong empirical support for peer support strategies indicates that they are an effective and practical approach for promoting access to the general curriculum and peer interactions among students with and without severe disabilities. The remaining chapters in this book focus on providing you with the guidance and tools needed for you to implement these strategies in your classrooms.

3

Crafting Effective Support Plans

Times are certainly changing at Castle High School. Over the past few years, the school has received considerable attention for its high dropout rates and failure to make adequate yearly progress, fueling calls from parents and school board members to explore new models for meeting the educational needs of students. A new principal—Dr. Lunsford—recently was hired to lead these efforts and to ensure that every student graduates from Castle with a strong foundation for success. One of her primary emphases was making certain that every student has access to a rigorous, relevant curriculum and receives the supports he or she needs to meet these high expectations. And when Dr. Lunsford spoke about all students, she really meant all students. She was convinced that general and special educators should work together to provide strong teaching and instructional methods to students within the general education curriculum. Ms. Souza, a special educator, wondered what this would mean for her students. After all, students with severe disabilities at Castle traditionally had few opportunities to enroll in general education classes, especially academic classes like science, history, and language arts. She agreed with the vision Dr. Lunsford had laid out for the staff but knew a different approach to teaming and planning would be needed if inclusion were to be successful for her students. Ms. Souza decided she would begin by talking with Mr. Jakowski, a popular social studies teacher. He had a reputation as an engaging teacher and had always shown a willingness to work collaboratively with special education. Perhaps they could work together on a plan for including one of her students in his class during the spring semester.

Meaningful inclusion is built on a foundation of intentional planning. It requires consideration of a range of issues, including the content standards addressed within a classroom, the curricula used to cover these standards, the approaches used to deliver instruction, and the ways students will access the curriculum. It also requires consideration of the expectations teachers hold for students, the efforts needed to foster relationships and promote belonging, and the ways in which progress will be assessed. Such planning is best done within a collaborative approach in which general and special educators work together to plan for general education access (Jitendra, Edwards, Choutka, & Treadway, 2002; Kennedy & Fisher, 2001). Such thoughtful planning is an essential first step toward ensuring that students with severe disabilities access rigorous, relevant learning experiences and benefit fully from the myriad social opportunities available within inclusive classrooms. Indeed, peer support strategies will be most effective when implemented within classrooms informed by these planning efforts.

As mentioned in previous chapters, legislative and policy initiatives—such as the Individuals with Disabilities Education Improvement Act of 2004 (PL 108-446), the No Child Left Behind Act of 2001 (PL 107-110), and the President's Commission on Excellence in Special Education (2002)—are calling on schools to think differently about where students with severe disabilities spend their school day and the curricular standards by which they receive instruction. At the same time, these changes have direct implications for special educators, challenging them to explore new approaches to planning that attend to a broader range of factors (Clayton, Burdge, Denham, Kleinert, & Kearns, 2006; Cushing, Clark, Carter, & Kennedy, 2005). For example, special educators should now 1) understand the grade-level content standards guiding instruction within general education classroom (Browder & Spooner, 2006; Browder, Wakeman, et al., 2007); 2) be familiar with the routines, activities, expectations, and assessments commonly used by teachers within these environments (Janney & Snell, 2004); 3) determine how to embed students' individualized goals within these classrooms in ways that facilitate their academic and social development (Agran et al., 2002; Kennedy & Fisher, 2001); and 4) decide on the most promising approaches for supporting students to access this curriculum, participate in class activities, and make progress on their IEP goals.

At the same time, general educators are being asked to assume a more prominent role in meeting the educational needs of a broader range of students—including students with severe disabilities—within their classrooms. To be effective in these roles, general educators must be familiar with students' strengths and needs, be knowledgeable about students' IEP goals, and be prepared to address these goals within ongoing instruction. They also must understand how to design learning experiences that enable students to access the curriculum in a variety of ways. And general educators should create opportunities for students to access supports that encourage relationships and promote a sense of belonging for all students. It is clear that successful planning efforts must incorporate the perspectives and recommendations of general educators.

This evolution in service delivery also has implications for paraprofessionals. Researchers and advocates are calling for paraprofessionals to assume new roles and responsibilities within inclusive classrooms (Carter & Kennedy, 2006; Giangreco et al., 2004). To do so effectively, paraprofessionals must clearly understand the learning experiences and outcomes most important for the students whom they support.

In this chapter, we stress the importance of collaboration and describe one approach that general educators, special educators, and paraprofessionals can use to create meaningful plans for supporting the academic and social participation of students with severe disabilities in general education classrooms (Cushing et al., 2005). This process involves detailing 1) the specific standards informing curricula, instruction, and assessment; 2) the classroom expectations teachers hold for students; 3) the IEP goals students will work toward; and 4) the approaches used to support students in the array of learning opportunities existing within a classroom. Such an approach to planning will assist educators in more closely aligning the instruction and supports that students with disabilities receive with the learning experiences provided to other students in the classroom. When students with and without severe disabilities are working together on common activities toward shared goals, they are much more likely to have opportunities to learn from and get to know one another. Peer support strategies should be embedded within this planning process. In other words, one important aspect of planning for general education access involves identifying the ways in which peers will provide academic and social support to their classmates with severe disabilities.

Although we discuss each step in this planning process separately, it is important to emphasize at the outset that good planning is ongoing and fluid. At the beginning of the semester, planning teams may meet to identify which grade-level standards will be addressed in a classroom; identify any expectations related to class participation; determine which IEP goals will be addressed within the classroom; and decide how peers, paraprofessionals, educators, and other staff (e.g., related services providers) will be involved in supporting students with severe disabilities (see Behind the Strategies on p. 28). These initial conversations, however, may need to be revisited periodically throughout the school year as class schedules fluctuate,

When students with and without severe disabilities are working together on common activities toward shared goals, they are much more likely to have opportunities to learn from and get to know one another.

the curriculum changes, new instructional approaches are tried, additional IEP goals are introduced, or new support needs emerge. A static or "one-shot" approach to planning overlooks the fact that good teaching is dynamic and responsive to students' needs.

IDENTIFYING GRADE-LEVEL STANDARDS

For most of the past 3 decades, a functional curriculum approach has comprised the dominant service delivery model for educating students with severe disabilities (Browder & Cooper-Duffy, 2003; Browder & Spooner, 2006). This approach has largely emphasized teaching skills that are age appropriate, useful in everyday life, and contribute to greater school and community participation (Brown, Branston, Hamre-Nietupski, Johnson, et al., 1979; Ford et al., 1989). For example, teachers often focus instruction on vocational, recreational, daily living, and community skills considered functional within the environments in which students *are* participating (current environments) and eventually *will* participate (future environments). Although an emphasis on teaching functional skills should remain an important element of recommended practices for serving students with severe disabilities, schools are now being called on to expand their emphasis to instruction addressing academic skills and content directly anchored to general curriculum.

This emphasis on promoting access to the general curriculum has been fueled by recent standards-based reform efforts. As Wehmeyer and Field (2007, p. 14) noted, districts and states must now establish academic content standards (i.e., "knowledge, skills, and understanding that students should accomplish in specific content domains") and student achievement standards (i.e., "levels of achievement that exemplify proficiency, typically sequenced by grade or age") that *all* students are expected to work toward. In other words, local and state grade-level standards must now inform the curricula, instruction, and assessment strategies delivered within general education classrooms. At the same time, schools are now held accountable for ensuring that all students—including students with severe disabilities—are able to access and make progress toward these shared learning standards.

Behind the Strategies

Collaborating to Promote General Education Access

Although successful inclusion depends on team members working well together (Hunt, Doering, Hirose-Hatae, Maier, & Goetz, 2001; Hunt, Soto, Maier, & Doering, 2003), this emphasis on teamwork and collaboration in education is relatively new. Traditional models for educating students relied on two separate systems—general education and special education—creating an environment in which educators worked in relative isolation (Skrtic, 1991). The primary responsibilities of general and special educators involved teaching "their" students, whereas paraprofessionals were primarily limited to assisting special educators. Current educational practice emphasizes integrating the two systems (Rice, Drame, Owens, & Frattura, 2007). In fact, the President's Commission on Excellence in Special Education stated that "general education and special education share responsibilities for children with disabilities. They are not separate at any level—cost, instruction or even identification" (2002, p. 7). This thrust for more inclusive services requires educators to alter how they support students. Special educators are being called on to collaborate with others as their roles shift from primarily teaching to coordinating and consultation services (Mills, 1994; Stainback, Stainback, & Harris, 1989). Special educators have also witnessed a corresponding decrease in the amount of direct support they provide students with disabilities (Ferguson & Ralph, 1996). General educators now teach all students, including students with severe disabilities, in their classrooms. Correspondingly, the influx of professionals and paraprofessionals into their classrooms to support students with disabilities has changed the nature of classroom teaching. For general educators, special educators, paraprofessionals, and related services providers, such changes require exploring new strategies enabling them to work more cohesively. Within inclusive schools, the need for educators to collaborate effectively is critical.

This new emphasis on aligning instruction with state and local content standards has several potential benefits. First, the general education classroom is increasingly being identified as the preferred context for promoting access to the general curriculum for students with severe disabilities (Wehmeyer & Agran, 2006). After all, it is within these classrooms that the general curriculum is being taught by highly qualified teachers. Second, ensuring that all students work toward a shared set of learning standards contributes to higher expectations for students with severe disabilities (Browder et al., 2003; Browder et al., 2006; Clayton et al., 2006; Wehmeyer, Sands, Knowlton, & Kozleski, 2002). Third, this emphasis on shared standards makes it more possible for students with and without severe disabilities to work together on shared learning tasks. It is extremely difficult to promote cooperative work and peer interactions when students with and without disabilities are working on entirely different learning activities.

Understanding what all students in a particular class are expected to learn can help guide general and special educators in determining how students with severe disabilities will access this same curriculum. Therefore, an initial step in the planning process involves identifying the specific grade-level standards addressed within a particular classroom and considering how students with severe disabilities will meet each standard. Special and general educators should discuss the content to be covered during the semester, specifying which standards will be addressed and how. Once these overarching goals are identified, discussion can next turn to the ways in which students with severe disabilities will meet each standard, as well as whether any of these expectations may need to be modified. As educators negotiate which standards will be emphasized for students with severe disabilities, it is helpful to consider those standards most likely to further other valued outcomes, such as self-determination, peer relationships, and increased independence. For example, understanding the U.S. system of government may increase a student's understanding of basic rights (e.g., voting, citizenship), self-advocacy, and self-determination. Similarly, standards related to oral communication might provide a context for a student to practice important social-related skills.

We opened this chapter with a brief vignette about Castle High School. We revisit this example throughout the chapter to illustrate how this planning process might be used to promote general education access and to identify avenues through which peers can provide academic and social supports. Ramon is a junior at Castle High School and is one of Ms. Souza's students. He loves history, is an emerging self-advocate, and is very interested in getting to know more of his peers. So, it made sense to consider enrolling Ramon in Mr. Jakowski's U.S. government class for the spring semester. Although Mr. Jakowski had never had a student with multiple disabilities in any of his classes before, he was willing to take on the challenge of working with Ms. Souza to figure out how to meaningfully include Ramon, who uses an AAC device and a wheelchair, in this class.

Prior to the start of the spring semester, the two teachers met to discuss how they would support Ramon's enrollment in the U.S. government class. They began by reviewing some of the state content standards Mr. Jakowski would address during the semester and identifying key unit objectives. Both teachers understood the importance of making sure Ramon would be working toward learning outcomes consistent with those of his peers. They also recognized, however, that some of the ways in which Ramon would demonstrate attainment of these standards would be somewhat different than his peers. Mr. Jakowski explained that he expected to address several state standards in his class over the course of the semester, including ensuring that students

- Understand political systems, with an emphasis on the United States
- Understand events, trends, individuals and movements shaping the history of the state and the United States
- Understand world geography and the effects of geography on society, with an emphasis on the United States
- Listen and speak effectively in a variety of situations
- Write to communicate for a variety of purposes

Mr. Jakowski then showed Ms. Souza several unit objectives directly aligned with the grade-level standard related to understanding political systems in the United States. To ensure that his students understand the basic principles of the government, Mr. Jakowski designed instructional activities to help students meet the following objectives:

- Students will describe the three branches of government and their primary responsibilities.
- Students will describe the system of checks and balances among these three branches and explain the purpose of sharing powers.
- Students will explain the emergence of the two-party system.
- Students will identify challenges associated with the two-party system.

Next, Ms. Souza and Mr. Jakowski discussed the modifications Ramon might need to meet these standards and unit objectives. It was clear Ramon would experience some difficulty meeting all of these objectives in exactly the same way as his peers. At the same time, both teachers thought that the essential concepts underlying these objectives were important for Ramon to learn. Ramon would soon be eligible to vote and had expressed an interest in becoming a self-advocate. Therefore, the two teachers decided Ramon should be expected to 1) name the three main branches of government, 2) name the current president and vice president of the United States, and 3) distinguish between the two main political parties.

By identifying in advance the standards Ramon would be expected to meet within Mr. Jakowski's history class, the teachers were able to come to consensus on which learning outcomes would be most important for Ramon. Ms. Souza gained a better understanding of the specific standards and unit objectives that would be emphasized during the semester, enabling her to start thinking in advance about the adaptations and modifications Ramon might need to be successful within the class next semester. This also would allow her time to discuss with Ms. Rogers the supports that Ms. Rogers would provide to Ramon as a paraprofessional. Likewise, Mr. Jakowski now felt more confident about the modifications Ramon might need to participate in the class.

IDENTIFYING CLASSROOM EXPECTATIONS

The next step in the planning process involves gathering information about the specific expectations teachers hold for students across typical activities and routines within their classrooms. Every class in a school looks different, and every teacher holds somewhat different expectations for students. Indeed, a particular teacher may even hold different expectations for each of his or her classes across the school day. For example, teachers may rely on a common set of instructional approaches (e.g., class discussions, small-group projects, lecture) in each of their classrooms, have well-defined routines they expect students to follow, or require students to bring specific materials to class each day. It is important that special educators and paraprofessionals be familiar with these activities and routines so that they can 1) plan in advance for how students with severe disabilities will meet these expectations and 2) determine the supports students will need to do so. Knowing in advance which activities occur on a fairly consistent basis decreases the likelihood that decisions about needed adaptations and supports will be made "on the fly." Such discussions can also identify avenues through which peers can provide academic and social support to their classmates. General educators should not assume that other staff providing support within the classroom would automatically know what is expected.

One avenue for identifying these classroom expectations involves completing a *classroom activities assessment* (Cushing et al., 2005; Janney & Snell, 2004). Such a tool can help teams document information related to the 1) extent to which various instructional formats are used (e.g., class discussion, small-group projects, silent reading, independent seatwork), 2) avenues through which student progress typically is assessed (e.g., homework assignments, weekly quizzes, end-of-unit tests), 3) materials students need to participate fully in class (e.g., textbooks, planners, calculators, computers), 4) types of assistance the teacher typically provides to students, and 5) rules and routines students are expected to follow. These expectations all combine to create a unique classroom environment. Some of these typical activities and routines will encourage the full participation of all students; others will stand as potential barriers unless effective adaptations and supports are implemented. Gathering this information in advance enables planning teams to be proactive in ensuring students have the supports needed to be successful—academically and socially—within the classroom.

Figure 3.1 displays a completed Classroom Activities Assessment form for Ramon. In the first column, the team lists the typical activities and routines taking place within the classroom related to 1) whole-class instruction, 2) small-group instruction, 3) independent work, 4) homework, 5) assessment, 6) needed materials, and 7) other expectations. In the second column, the team briefly describe its expectations for all students across each of these activities and routines. In the third column, the team outlines the possible adaptations and supports that a student with severe disabilities might need to participate meaningfully in each of these activities and routines. For example, peer support strategies are often listed here as an approach for helping students participate more fully in class activities. When each of these issues is discussed collaboratively among general educators, special educators, and paraprofessionals supporting students within the classroom, it clarifies for everyone exactly how students will participate socially and academically within the classroom. To help you use this tool in your classroom, a blank photocopiable version of this form is available in the appendix at the end of this book.

Classroom Activities Assessment

Class: _U.S. government/11th grade_   Student: _Ramon_

Teacher: _Mr. Jakowski_   Team: _Mr. Jakowski, Ms. Souza, and Ms. Rogers_

Typical activities and routines	Expectations for students	Adaptations and supports
Lecture	Students listen, answer questions, and take notes (3x–4x per week).	R will sit in the front of the class-room; peers can share notes; R will follow along with guided notes; teacher and/or peers will ask R clari-fying questions.
Current events discussion	Students share info from newspa-pers, Internet, radio, and TV related to current political events covered in class (daily).	As during lecture, R will sit in the front of the classroom.
Watching documentaries	Students complete guided notes cre-ated by the teachers; discussion follows (2x per month).	R will complete guided notes adapted to stress main concepts/ideas; R will review what he watched with his peer supports.
Guest speakers	Local and state representatives talk about being a public official; students must research each speaker prior to each talk and prepare questions about current events (3x per semester).	R will research upcoming guest speakers with a peer on the Internet; peers will identify topic ideas for R to search; peers will help R program questions into his AAC device.
Cooperative learning groups	Students review information covered during the week and answer work-sheet questions (1x per week).	Adapted questions for R should have two- to three-sentence answers; peers can check sentences to ensure correct spelling and grammar.
Debate teams	Students are asked to research both sides of a current topic and debate the issue in teams (1x per month).	Peers supports can help R enter key arguments into his AAC device for the group; R's role will be to start the debate.
Worksheets	Students use their textbook to answer worksheet questions (2x–3x per week).	R will use guided notes that stress main concepts; he will select cor-rect answers from three multiple choices; peers can assist him when done with their work.

(continued)

Figure 3.1.   Classroom Activities Assessment for Ramon. A blank version of this form appears in the appendix at the end of this book. (From Janney, R., & Snell, M.E. [2004]. *Modifying schoolwork* [p. 64]. Baltimore: Paul H. Brookes Publishing Co.; adapted by permission.)

Figure 3.1.   *(continued)*

Typical activities and routines	Expectations for students	Adaptations and supports
Silent reading/ research	Students read about current events at their desk or on the computer when finished with worksheets (2x–3x per week).	R can work with peers to search info on the computer or listen to his textbook chapters on the computer.
Textbook readings	Students read approximately one chapter per week.	R will listen to each assigned chapter aloud on the computer.
Current events summaries	Students compose one-paragraph written summaries of current issues in the news (3x per week).	R will compile typed summaries from various web-based news organizations.
Unit tests	Complete multiple-choice and essay exams (1x per month).	Response options will be reduced to three choices; only three sentences required for essay questions; answers can be read by and dictated to a paraprofessional.
Quizzes	Complete multiple-choice and short answer questions (2x per month).	Same as for tests
Worksheets	Answer questions related to lecture and/or readings (2x–3x per week).	R can work together with one of his peer supports to complete the worksheets.
Debate performance	Students are evaluated on their command of the topic and adherence to debate rules (1x per month).	R will work with peers to prepare key arguments.
Textbook	Needed daily	R will need access to an electronic version.
Guided notes	3x–4x per week	R's guided notes will contain fewer items.
Paper, pen, planner	Needed daily	No adaptations/supports
Come to class prepared and ready to learn	Students are expected to arrive before the bell, turn in assignments on time, and come prepared for discussions.	R will make his way to class with a peer.
Be respectful	Students expected to raise their hands before speaking.	R will use an adapted switch.
Bathroom breaks	Students ask for a pass from a teacher.	R is accompanied by a paraprofessional.

The information needed to complete this classroom activities assessment can be gathered in a variety of ways. First, general educators can independently complete the first two columns, writing down their expectations for students across typical activities and routines. Special educators and paraprofessionals can then use this information to begin planning the adaptations and supports students will need to benefit fully from the learning experiences and peer interaction opportunities available within the classroom. Second, special educators or paraprofessionals can observe in the classroom over several class periods at the beginning of the school year or during the prior semester to record information about how students typically are involved in the class. After brainstorming ideas for adaptations and supports to enhance a student's participation, they might meet with the classroom teachers to discuss further these initial ideas. Third, planning teams can all meet prior to the start of the semester to work through the planning tool together. This last approach is likely to be most productive, as it provides an opportunity for all staff working in the classroom to talk through each activity, ask questions, and creatively generate strategies for more closely aligning the learning experiences of students with and without severe disabilities.

Before the start of the semester, Ms. Souza and Mr. Jakowski met together to complete a classroom activities assessment for Ramon. Because Ms. Rogers would also be working in the classroom as a paraprofessional and had provided individualized support to Ramon in the past, they asked her to be part of the discussion. The following sections describe some of the issues they discussed and strategies they considered.

Instructional Formats

Mr. Jakowski uses a variety of instructional approaches within his classroom during a typical semester. For example, he often lectures for 15–20 minutes at the beginning of class to provide students with the background information needed to complete their assignments or to expand on topics addressed in the textbook readings. These lectures are usually followed by whole-class discussions linking current political events in the news to the overarching unit topic. Periodically, Mr. Jakowski also shows short clips from documentaries or invites local government officials to speak to the class. Students regularly work in small groups of three to five classmates to discuss current issues, complete worksheet assignments, and prepare for upcoming class debates.

As they discussed these typical instructional formats, Ms. Souza felt confident that Ramon could participate in each of these activities if he were provided with some adaptations and supports. For example, during lectures and class discussions, she suggested that Ramon sit toward the front of the classroom to minimize potential distractions and to ensure that he could hear the lecture and subsequent discussion. She also recommended he work with one or more peers during this time who could share their notes, summarize key points, and encourage Ramon to ask or answer questions when appropriate. Ms. Souza felt this would increase the opportunities Ramon had to interact with and get to know his classmates, as well as decrease his reliance on Ms. Rogers for help. Ms. Souza also thought Ramon would be more engaged if he was asked clarifying questions by Mr. Jakowski or peers to reinforce the main points of the discussion. When Mr. Jakowski asked how Ramon would participate in class discussions on current events, Ms. Rogers suggested Ramon could search the Internet for stories addressing local political issues and bring in examples relevant to the class discussion.

Mr. Jakowski suggested that other students in the cooperative group could easily assist Ramon with his assignments by helping him check for spelling and grammar errors before he turned them in. Usually, one or two students finish their work early and could easily assume this role. When preparing for class debates, Ms. Souza indicated that Ramon could type the team's opening argument into his augmentative and alternative communication (AAC) device with help from his peers. Ramon would assume primary responsibility for launching the debate, giving him an important and valued role on his team while allowing him to be able to prepare ahead of time. Other team members would be responsible for making the follow-up arguments and closing statements.

Homework Assignments and Assessments

Like most teachers, Mr. Jakowski uses a variety of approaches to assess students' progress toward unit objectives and grade-level standards. For example, grades in his U.S. government class are based on students' performance on homework assignments, quizzes, unit tests, contributions to class discussion, and participation in class debates. Ms. Souza was excited to discover Mr. Jakowski had selected a textbook with universal design for learning components (Browder et al., 2006; Hitchcock, Meyer, Rose, & Jackson, 2002). Such textbooks are designed to meet the needs of students with diverse reading and academic levels by offering options on a CD or a web site to "read" the text aloud, define specific words, or explain concepts in greater detail. This electronic textbook would enable Ramon to keep up with reading assignments despite his limited reading skills.

At the end of each unit, Mr. Jakowski administers an exam consisting primarily of multiple-choice and essay questions. Based on her experiences in previous classes, Ms. Souza proposed reducing the number of response options for multiple-choice questions from five to three. She also recommended that Ms. Rogers or Mr. Jakowski read the questions aloud to Ramon or record them in advance so that Ramon could listen to them using a headset. The teachers also agreed that Ramon would only be able to provide two- or three-sentence answers for the essay sections of the exam and that these questions would need to be focused to emphasize those essential elements of the grade-level standards most important for Ramon to understand. Ms. Souza indicated she would modify each exam if Mr. Jakowski could provide them to her at least a couple of days in advance. This also would allow Mr. Jakowski to pass out the exams to all of the students in the classroom at the same time.

Rules and Other Expectations

Mr. Jakowski expects students in all of his classes to 1) arrive to class on time, 2) be in their seats before the bell rings, 3) raise their hands to ask questions or make comments, 4) turn in all homework and in-class assignments on-time, 5) keep abreast of current events related to the class readings, and 6) come to class ready to learn. Ms. Souza acknowledged the importance of these expectations for Ramon and believed that he would be able to meet them with some modifications. Instead of raising his hand to make a comment or ask for assistance—which was physically difficult—Ramon could activate a switch attached to the arm of his wheelchair. Mr. Jakowski was adamant that every student be at his or her desk by the time the bell rings, including Ramon. Ms. Souza explained that Ramon was often late because he had difficulty navigating the crowded hallways on his own and he was resistant to making his way to class with an adult. Mr. Jakowski suggested they find one or more peers who attended class with Ramon during the period prior to U.S. government who would be interested in walking with Ramon.

As the educators talked through each section of the classroom activities assessment tool, they were encouraged by how many opportunities existed for Ramon to work with and get to know his classmates. Peers would walk with Ramon to and from class, providing students with opportunities to get to know each other outside of class. This also gave Ramon the independence he wanted and kept him from always having to be accompanied by an adult. During class, peers would be identified who could help Ramon get to his desk, take out his materials for class, and participate more fully in various class activities. Almost of all of the typical activities and routines within Mr. Jakowski's class provided natural opportunities for peers to provide academic and social support to Ramon. For example, the team outlined a variety of ways that peers could provide assistance to Ramon during lectures, class discussions, guest speakers, small-group work, and independent seatwork. Because Mr. Jakowski frequently uses small-group formats during class—such as cooperative learning groups and debate teams—peers are already expected to work together and support each another. Identifying one or two peers from within Ramon's small group to provide a bit more intentional assistance would be a natural extension of what already occurs within these small groups.

Although the meeting took some time, Mr. Jakowski certainly appreciated having this discussion with Ms. Souza and Ms. Rogers. Initially, he had been unsure about what it would look like for Ramon to be included in his class. He now understood that Ramon would be working toward many of the same learning outcomes and general expectations Mr. Jakowski held for all of his students. Ms. Souza now had a much clearer understanding of what would be expected of Ramon in this class and could begin working with Ms. Rogers to plan how to support Ramon most effectively. And Ms. Rogers left much more certain about her future role within the classroom.

INFUSING INDIVIDUALIZED EDUCATION PROGRAM GOALS INTO GENERAL EDUCATION CLASSROOMS

As emphasized previously in this chapter, standards-based reforms are introducing new curricular expectations for students with severe disabilities by calling on schools to ensure that all students are making progress toward state and local content standards. At the same time, students with severe disabilities also are likely to have individualized goals not directly addressed within grade-level standards. For example, goals and objectives addressing functional skills in the domains of communication, behavior, daily living, self-determination, and mobility frequently are found on students' IEPs. Although many educators sense an underlying tension between this new emphasis on promoting content standards and the enduring emphasis on meeting the individualized goals of students, it is entirely possible to address both of these emphases simultaneously. In other words, many—if not all—of a student's IEP goals can be met within general education contexts, such as academic classrooms, electives, and extracurricular activities.

An *IEP matrix* can help planning teams determine where and how a student's individualized goals will be addressed within general education classes and other inclusive contexts throughout the school day (Kennedy & Fisher, 2001). Rather than set aside discrete times to work on students' goals in separate settings, team members should look for naturally occurring times, locations, and activities within which goals can be emphasized. When planning teams have already discussed the curricular standards, activities, routines, and expectations within general education classrooms, they are in a much better position to consider whether and how each of a student's IEP objectives and goals might be embedded within a particular classroom (see Behind the Strategies on this page). A completed IEP matrix clarifies for general educators,

Behind the Strategies

Embedding IEP Goals

Research suggests that students may be more likely to acquire skills outlined in their IEP goals when instruction is embedded within existing activities, rather than teaching skills in separate settings, out of their natural context, or by using massed trials (e.g., Agran, Cavin, Wehmeyer, & Palmer, 2006; McDonnell, Johnson, Polychronis, & Risen, 2002; Wolery, Anthony, Snyder, Werts, & Katzenmeyer, 1997). For example, if students have IEP goals addressing social interaction and communication skills, it makes sense to focus on promoting these skills within environments offering frequent, natural opportunities for students to interact with their peers, such as during group projects in class, in the hallways, at lunch, or within extracurricular activities. Such contexts offer numerous opportunities for students to practice social and communication skills with their peers and to receive reinforcement for using those skills appropriately. Embedding IEP goal instruction throughout the day also provides students with multiple opportunities to practice skills in a variety of contexts, increasing the likelihood students will maintain their skills over time and generalize their skills to other environments.

special educators, and paraprofessionals which goals are—and are not—most important to address within a particular classroom. At the same time, the matrix helps ensure specific IEP goals are not being overlooked during the school day.

Figure 3.2 displays the IEP Matrix form that Ms. Souza and Ms. Rogers drafted after talking with each of Ramon's general education teachers. Ramon's abbreviated goals and objectives are listed down the left column of the matrix. Teachers may choose to list all of a student's goals and objectives or to prioritize only the most important ones. Listed along the top row are the classes and activities making up Ramon's daily schedule. When listing environments, consider the full range of contexts within which students spend their school day, including lunch, extracurricular clubs, breaks, community-based experiences, or service-learning projects. As each goal and environment is discussed, educators check off boxes to indicate when and where each IEP goal will be addressed. For your use, a photocopiable, blank version of this form can be found in the appendix at the end of this book.

> *Many—if not all—of a student's IEP goals can be met within general education contexts, such as academic classrooms, electives, and extracurricular activities.*

After completing the classroom activities assessment, Ms. Souza discussed several of Ramon's IEP goals with Mr. Jakowski. Specifically, she identified six skills as priority goals:

- Using his motorized wheelchair to independently navigate his environment
- Answering questions (using his AAC device) posed to him by peers and adults
- Appropriately asking for needed assistance from peers or adults
- Writing paragraphs of two or more sentences in length using correct spelling and grammar

IEP Matrix

Student: _Ramon_   Semester/school year: _Spring 2009_

Individualized goals	Home-room	U.S. government	Study hall	English	Computer science	Lunch	Math	General science	Clubs
Using his motorized wheelchair to independently navigate his environment	X	X	X	X	X	X	X	X	X
Answering questions (using his AAC device) posed to him by peers and adults	X	X	X	X	X	X	X	X	X
Appropriately asking for needed assistance from peers and adults	X	X	X	X	X	X	X	X	X
Writing paragraphs of two or more sentences in length with correct spelling and grammar		X		X				X	
Correctly answering content-related questions posed by peers or adults		X		X	X		X	X	
Responding appropriately to social greetings from peers	X	X	X	X	X	X	X	X	X

Daily schedule

Figure 3.2.   Ramon's IEP Matrix. A blank version of this form appears in the appendix at the end of this book. (*Source:* Kennedy & Fisher, 2001.)

- Correctly answering content-related questions posed by peers or adults
- Responding appropriately to social greetings from peers

As Ms. Souza explained Ramon's goals, she and Mr. Jakowski brainstormed ways each goal could be addressed within the context of the U.S. government class. For example, both teachers agreed that Ramon could work on his social-related goals across a variety of classroom activities. Students typically converse with each other before the bell rings and after they finish their work for the day, providing numerous opportunities for Ramon to greet and get to know peers he did not know from other classes. Small-group activities and the debate teams provided natural opportunities for students to ask each other questions, work collaboratively on shared tasks, and reinforce important curricular content. Mr. Jakowski also explained that during lectures and whole-class discussions, he regularly asks students questions to make sure they understood the material. He agreed to use this opportunity to ask Ramon questions related to the course content, as well as to encourage the peers providing support to Ramon's to do the same. Ms. Souza emphasized she wanted Ramon to become more fluent with using his AAC device during interactions with teachers and classmates. She felt Ms. Rogers could play an important role in modeling for others how to support Ramon in using his AAC device.

The Embedded Goals Chart shown in Figure 3.3 highlights some of the ways the planning team decided to address Ramon's individualized goals within the U.S. government class. Both teachers agreed that several opportunities existed to address all six goals. Of course, instruction would not be limited to just these goals. Ramon would still be expected to make progress toward the grade-level standards that Mr. Jakowski, Ms. Souza, and Ms. Rogers had discussed. But the template provided Mr. Jakowski with a clearer understanding of other learning outcomes that were important for Ramon to attain within his classroom. (A blank version of this template appears in the appendix at the end of this book.)

Although embedding existing IEP goals within general education classes is an important aspect of good planning, educational teams should also consider how they might begin writing IEPs that more directly align *both* with students' individual educational priorities *and* with the general curriculum (Flowers, Browder, Ahlgrim-Delzell, & Spooner, 2006). In other words, teams can select goals relevant to the general education context and that directly tie to the same state standards applicable to other students in the class. Such standards-based IEPs have the advantage of reducing the perceived disconnect between the educational needs of students with severe disabilities and their classmates (Ahearn, 2006; Courtade-Little & Browder, 2005).

CONCLUSION

It is important to note that successful plans address academic *and* social learning opportunities. This chapter has described basic steps planning teams can take to enhance the student's ability to meaningfully access and progress in the general education curriculum. Statewide standards should be the foundation for the general curriculum and guide instruction for all students. Gathering information about the general education teacher's unit goals and classroom expectations can assist special educators to identify critical components of a general education classroom. Special education teachers gain a sense of the general education classroom environment and the kinds of skills the student with disabilities will need to learn to be successful in that classroom. It is also important to identify which IEP goals can be easily incorporated within the classroom context. Providing students with disabilities multiple opportunities to practice goals within natural environments increases the likelihood the student will learn the skill. As educa-

Embedded Goals Chart

Class: _U.S. government/11th grade_   Student: _Ramon_

Teacher: _Mr. Jakowski_   Team: _Mr. Jakowski, Ms. Souza, and Ms. Rogers_

Priority goals	When can this goal be addressed	How will progress be evaluated?
Using his motorized wheel-chair to independently navigate his environment	Entering and exiting the class-room; moving around the class-room between activities or during small-group projects	Classroom observations; num-ber of days he arrives to class on time from attendance records
Answering questions (using his AAC device) posed to him by peers and adults	Conversations with peers before/after class and when work is completed; discussions within small groups and debate teams; interactions with peers; at least two questions from Mr. Jakowski each class period	Classroom observations by the paraprofessional
Appropriately asking for needed assistance from peers and adults	When completing guided notes, researching questions for guest speakers, completing worksheets, and preparing for class debates; when needing a bathroom break	Classroom observations by the paraprofessional
Writing paragraphs of two or more sentences in length with correct spelling and grammar	During cooperative learning groups; preparing debate argu-ments; current event summaries homework; unit tests	Examination of worksheets, homework assignments, and unit tests
Correctly answering content-related questions posed by peers or adults	With peer supports during lec-tures and current event discus-sions; discussions within small groups and debate teams; at least two questions from Mr. Jakowski each class period	Classroom observations by the paraprofessional
Responding appropriately to social greetings from peers	Interactions with peers before/after class and once classwork is completed	Classroom observations by the paraprofessional

Figure 3.3. Ramon's IEP goals addressed within the U.S. government class. A blank version of this form appears in the appendix at the end of this book.

tors plan for a student's meaningful inclusion, they must also consider strategies that enhance the student's ability to interact with peers. Strategies such as peer supports are especially impor-tant for inclusive classrooms. These approaches tap into an existing resource that is commonly underutilized. Peers can be used to supplement a student's academic program and to facilitate social interactions with peers. The key component involves thoughtful planning. Success is highly dependent on planning ahead. That is, the more a collaborative team plans for the aca-demic and social success of a student with severe disabilities, the better the outcomes.

4

Identifying Peer Support Participants

Yvonne was finally going to be a freshman at Goodman High School. The beginning of the school year offered her a fresh start and exciting opportunities to meet new friends, take interesting classes, and get more involved in her school. She was finally in high school and she was going to make the most of it! For the first week of school—as she had throughout all of middle school—Yvonne attended classes accompanied by a paraprofessional. Although Yvonne had some difficulty articulating it in words, it quickly became clear to the teachers that having to "hang out" with an adult each class period "cramped her style." Yvonne's teachers realized that a different support model would be needed, so they decided to try peer support strategies. Although new to Goodman, Yvonne did know one other classmate fairly well from her previous middle school. Although Tenecia was neither the highest achiever nor the most popular student in the class, she and Yvonne had many things in common—including the fact that they both lived in the same neighborhood and were huge college basketball fans. Unfortunately, Yvonne was never asked who she wanted to work with. Instead, she was paired with another classmate who, although academically strong, was not particularly well known to Yvonne. The peer support arrangement worked out okay, but it was far from stellar. Although Yvonne seemed to appreciate having help from someone other than a paraprofessional, the classmates to whom her peer introduced her really were not people she was interested in being friends with. And many of the early hopes Yvonne had for her new school year were not materializing.

Schools are rich reservoirs of natural support. And, students are often among the most overlooked and underutilized avenues for supporting inclusive education on any elementary, middle, or high school campus. Whether in the classroom, during extracurricular and other school activities, throughout lunch, or between classes, students can be seen working together, hanging out, and exchanging a wide array of academic, social, emotional, material, and other types of support. Indeed, students supporting their peers is a normative experience in schools—whether formally arranged by teachers or informally negotiated by students. For students with severe disabilities, drawing upon these natural sources of peer support has the potential to enhance their learning opportunities, expand their social experiences, and improve the overall quality of their education experience.

Determining which classmates will make the most effective peer supports for a particular student with disabilities, however, is not always readily apparent. As illustrated with Yvonne, identifying a student to provide support is only part of the equation. Finding a good match—students who are likely to work well together in ways that are mutually beneficial and promote reciprocal relationships—requires thoughtful consideration. What factors might contribute to successful peer support arrangements? The students with and without disabilities who participate, the history they share, the degree to which they work well together, and their personal investment in their new roles can all influence the outcomes students attain. In this chapter, we offer guidance on how educators can identify students—with and without severe disabilities—who might benefit most from involvement in peer support interventions. Although there is no single "right" way to identify peer supports and to structure peer support arrangements—no infallible set of steps will guarantee success—research on peer relationships and inclusive education provides valuable guidance on strategies to pursue and pitfalls to avoid. Therefore, we discuss a variety of approaches educators might take when beginning this process.

CHARACTERISTICS OF EFFECTIVE PEER SUPPORTS AND GOOD PEER SUPPORT MATCHES

Prior to involving general education students in peer support interventions, it is important to have some ideas about the qualities and characteristics that participating students should exhibit (Cowie & Wallace, 2000). What should educators look for when identifying students to serve as peer supports? Are there essential qualities that peers should possess? What skills or traits typically characterize an effective peer? The answers to these questions might be influenced by multiple considerations, including your expectations for the peer support experience; the specific outcomes that you are hoping students with and without disabilities will attain; the grade level at which you teach (i.e., elementary, middle, or high school); the environments within which students with disabilities will need support; the educational goals of participating students; and, of course, the personal preferences of the participating students. For example, if the primary purpose is to expand students' friendship networks and strengthen their social connections in specific classes, you may invite different students as peer supports than if your primary goal is more academically oriented.

Educators should consider and weigh several factors when identifying and selecting potential peer supports and should identify which of these factors are most relevant in light of the curricular, social, or other expectations of the particular classroom or school environment. An initial set of peer support considerations should be developed, all of which can later be refined over time as educators gain more experience implementing peer support arrangements in their classrooms. The following factors might be considered when identifying peer supports for students with severe disabilities. Although these attributes do not necessarily all have to be apparent in every peer, we discuss the possible impact educators might expect when each factor is or is not considered.

Preference of Students with Disabilities

What ought to be among the first questions asked is too often never even raised: Whom does the student with disabilities want to work together with, spend time with, and develop a potential friendship with? Historically, students with severe disabilities have infrequently been given opportunities to provide meaningful input into their own education programming and the supports they receive (Martin, Van Dycke, Christensen, et al., 2006; Test et al., 2004). Broer and colleagues (2005) asked youth and young adults with intellectual disabilities to reflect on the supports they received during high school and found that many of these students had limited input on who provided support and the manner in which it was delivered. To the greatest extent possible, the preferences of students with disabilities should be considered when identifying potential peer supports—whether the focus of support is primarily academic, social, vocational, or something else.

All students—particularly during adolescence—have clear preferences about the peers with whom they want to spend time, and having a significant disability does not diminish this reality. Moreover, if fostering friendships is a desired goal of peer support arrangements, it is essential to consider the preferences of the student with disabilities. Ask the student if there are particular classmates with whom he or she would like to partner during the semester, peers whom the student particularly likes or has expressed an interest in getting to know better. For students with limited communication skills, educators will need to employ creative strategies to discern students' preferences (see Cannella, O'Reilly, & Lancioni, 2005; Lohrmann-O'Rourke, Browder, & Brown, 2000). For example, teachers might 1) observe carefully to see which classmates a student seems to gravitate toward, 2) have the student select from among pictures of his or her classmates from a yearbook, or 3) give the student the opportunity to work with small groups of classmates to determine whom he or she "clicks" with. For students who have experienced a history of limited inclusion and who have few or no social connections within their school, it will be important that teachers not interpret this isolation as a lack of desire to get to know their classmates.

What ought to be among the first questions asked is too often never even raised: Whom does the student with disabilities want to work together with, spend time with, and develop a potential friendship with?

Similar Ages

Some peer-mediated interventions—such as cross-age tutoring—involve older students in providing academic support to younger students (e.g., Robinson, Schofield, & Steers-Wentzell, 2005; Spencer, 2006). For example, high schools often rely heavily on juniors and seniors within peer tutor or peer mentor programs because their course schedules typically offer greater flexibility. Participants in peer support programs, however, generally should be invited from among same-age peers who are enrolled within the same classrooms as the students with disabilities (see the section called Strategies for Identifying Peers later in this chapter). Indeed, it is typical for adolescents to seek out friendships with similar-age peers (Brown & Klute, 2003). Moreover, when peers are always substantially older, the likelihood that long-term friendships will emerge from these relationships may be reduced.

Expressed Interest

The most successful peer support arrangements are those in which all participating students are interested in and enthusiastic about working together. Not every student will want to be a peer support and no one should be compelled to assume this role if he or she is reluctant or simply does not have an interest. Students may decide not to become a peer support for several reasons (Carter et al., 2001; Siperstein, Norins, & Mohler, 2007). Although one might be tempted to suppose that these students hold negative attitudes about their classmates with disabilities, other factors may contribute to their reluctance, including uncertainty regarding their own ability to provide support, unfamiliarity with or limited information about the classmate with disabilities, concern that helping another person could cause them to fall behind academically, or altogether different and unarticulated reasons. As these students have the opportunity to observe other peers working with their classmate with disabilities over time, however, this initial hesitation may fade. Indeed, it may be that as students come to see their classmate with disabilities as having greater competence than they initially realized, these students may become more willing to interact with them during the school day (Siperstein, Parker, et al., 2007). The most common reason students do not get involved, however, is because they are never asked. Do not assume that because someone does not directly, independently approach you to serve as a peer support that they are not interested. Frequently "sticking up" for a student, asking questions about him or her, or making inquiries when he or she is not present in class may all be ways a classmate might be expressing an interest in getting to know a student better.

Consistent Attendance

Regular attendance may be among the most important characteristics of an effective peer support. Clearly, it is difficult for someone to provide support to their classmates when he or she is not present at school. Students with disabilities will come to rely on their peers for consistent academic, social, and other forms of support, particularly in classrooms or other contexts in which a paraprofessional or special educator is not present. Students with erratic attendance, even if they do an effective job when present, may inadvertently cause their classmate with disabilities to fall behind. The importance of consistent attendance highlights the potential value of involving more than one peer in these arrangements to ensure that support is consistently available (Carter, Cushing, et al., 2005).

As mentioned in Chapter 2, however, serving as a peer support may actually have a collateral benefit of increasing the school attendance for students who are at risk for dropping out by providing a highly reinforcing and personally meaningful role at school. In other words, for students struggling to find success in school and who feel disconnected from teachers, being a peer support sometimes provides a compelling reason to come to class because it increases positive contact with teachers and can contribute to a sense of personal accomplishment.

Shared Interests

Adolescents tend to develop relationships with others with whom they have something in common—a mutual interest in sports, a favorite band or style of music, a common hobby, a shared group of friends, similar religious beliefs, or living in the same neighborhood (Sussman, Pokhrel, Ashmore, & Brown, 2007). The more students hold in common, the more likely they will enjoy the time they spend together and, perhaps, the greater the likelihood they will develop relationships that extend outside of the classroom. If it is obvious that there are students with shared interests, consider asking them to become involved as peer supports. Keep in mind, however, that the things students share in common might not be readily apparent to adults from the outset. Quite often, as students spend time together and get to know each other, they may discover they hold more in common than they realized at first. In fact, participants in peer support arrangements frequently mention this unexpected discovery of mutual interests (Copeland et al., 2004). At the same time, it is important that special educators and paraprofessionals actually know what their students' interests are, as well as help them to develop further those age-appropriate interests that are likely to be held in common with classmates (Kluth & Schwarz, 2008).

Peers with Existing Social Networks

Educators often consider implementing peer support arrangements because of their potential for expanding students' friendships (Carter & Pesko, 2008; Copeland et al., 2002). Connecting students with severe disabilities with peers who themselves have a close network of friends can have the collateral benefit of introducing the students with disabilities to new and already existing networks of peers in the school (Kennedy, 2001; Schnorr, 1997). For example, Haring and Breen (1992) implemented a peer network intervention in which they specifically sought the involvement of general education students who had existing friendship networks into which students with severe disabilities could be introduced. These peers introduced their classmates into their friendship circles, expanding the number of new classmates with whom the student with disabilities regularly came into contact. The result of these efforts was substantial increases in peer interaction among students with and without disabilities.

Interestingly, becoming a peer support also may positively affect the social network of the student serving as a peer support. Particularly in the elementary and early middle school grades, additional social status sometimes is attached to serving in this role or in any other classroom role carrying teacher-assigned responsibilities (Coie, Dodge, & Kupersmidt, 1990). Similarly, at the high school level, classmates sometimes perceive students who serve in peer support roles more favorably. In schoolwide peer support programs, serving as a peer support also promotes relationships among the students in the school who are serving in the same role.

Interpersonal Skills

Peers are expected to work closely with their classmates with disabilities to promote academic participation and facilitate social interactions with other students in their school. Moreover, peers will need to communicate regularly about their roles, training needs, and any emerging challenges with teachers and paraprofessionals. Although having good interpersonal skills may be one of the less tangible of qualities to pinpoint, its importance should not be underestimated. For example, qualities such as friendliness, the ability to work cooperatively and get along with others, confidence, respect, empathy, and sensitivity can all enhance the success of peer support interventions.

Willingness to Learn

Most peers will need guidance—at least initially—concerning how to support their classmates with disabilities effectively (see Chapter 5, "Equipping Students to Provide Academic and Social Support"). Students who have demonstrated a willingness and eagerness to learn new skills, take initiative, and tackle new challenges may be especially effective as they assume these new roles.

Summary of Effective Supports and Good Matches

Although these recommendations emerge from our work with many students across myriad schools, it should be emphasized that identifying effective peer supports, as with facilitating friendships, can be as much art as science. Peer relationships—particularly during adolescence—often form or falter for reasons that are difficult for adults to understand. So, we stress this important caveat to these various recommendations: There is no magic formula for the perfect peer support arrangement. Some students may not possess all of these attributes and yet still make excellent peer supports. Similarly, educators simply may not realize that a student possesses these characteristics until he or she has been given an opportunity to demonstrate them. Therefore, what is critical is that educators regularly reflect on the education interventions they employ and evaluate whether those interventions are having the intended effects for participating students.

FACTORS MOTIVATING THE INVOLVEMENT OF STUDENTS

It is also worth considering what students find reinforcing and satisfying about their involvement in peer support initiatives. This information will not only provide guidance concerning how to invite new peers, but it also will be helpful for identifying approaches for maintaining students' continued involvement in these roles. What is it that motivates students to become involved in peer support activities? The answer likely varies from student to student, but it should not be automatically assumed that someone's only or primary motivation to volunteer is his or her desire to help a particular classmate with disabilities (Kennedy, 2002b).

Most students do choose to become involved in peer support programs simply because they recognize it as another opportunity to develop a new friendship or assist one of their classmates. As schools increasingly serve students with and without disabilities together in inclusive classrooms (Williamson et al., 2006), many of these students may already know each other and have had some opportunities to spend time together in the past. Other students have siblings or relatives with disabilities and feel very comfortable interacting with their classmates with disabilities. For example, they may recognize that a student with

We stress this important caveat: There is no magic formula for the perfect peer support arrangement.

disabilities in their class seems somewhat isolated and disconnected from his or her classmates and will take steps to encourage greater participation.

Other students, however, may become involved for altogether different reasons. For example, students may volunteer because the experience provides them with additional opportunities to interact with teachers and paraprofessionals, improves their social status among classmates, provides them access to a desired peer group, or contributes to the strength of their college application. They may also be committed to social justice issues and see this as a way to address participation and equity issues within their school and community.

What serves as a catalyst for students' initial decision to become a peer support often changes over time. As peers spend more time with and get to know their partners with disabilities, the underlying factors maintaining their involvement may evolve. For example, one student initially became a peer support as a way to have more access to teachers. After weeks of getting to know the classmate she was supporting, she found they shared much in common and she began to look forward to fifth period when they worked together in ecology class. Thus, we recommend that educators not be unduly concerned about students who initially begin with different motivations.

EXPANDING INVOLVEMENT TO A BROADER RANGE OF STUDENTS

In light of the clear social and academic benefits peer support arrangements hold for all students with *and* without disabilities, educators should think creatively about strategies for involving a broader spectrum of students in these programs. Which members of the student body traditionally have been involved in peer support activities? Typically, teachers tend to invite students who are female, who are achieving at or above grade level, who evidence very positive attitudes, and who do not have disabilities. Although the involvement of these students should certainly be encouraged, educators should explore strategies for expanding the range of students positively affected by participation in peer support interventions. Because of the substantial academic, social, and personal benefits that peers may accrue from their involvement in these arrangements (Carter & Kennedy, 2006; Jones, 2007; Longwill & Kleinert, 1998), it is important to think about how to involve students who might not otherwise participate or who historically have had limited participation.

Males

Peer support interventions often draw substantially higher involvement by females than males (e.g., Carter et al., 2001; Janney & Snell, 2006; Kishi & Meyer, 1994). Although the literature is not clear on why this is the case, possible explanations might include attitudinal differences among students (Krajewski & Flaherty, 2000; Siperstein, Norins, & Moehler, 2007), teachers' decisions about whom they invite, or differences in friendship expectations among girls and boys (Han & Chadsey, 2004). When taking into account students' preferences about who will provide them with support, remember that adolescents more often choose to develop friendships with same-gender peers (Brown & Klute, 2003). Thus, if one goal of peer support interventions is to increase interactions that extend beyond the classroom, it may be important to also seek same-gender students as potential peer supports.

Average-Achieving and At-Risk Students

Educators may be tempted to look first among academically promising students for potential participants. Such students often make excellent supports and may have greater flexibility in their work, allowing them to provide ongoing support to another classmate. However, limiting involvement to academically high achieving students overlooks the fact that a wide range of students can 1) benefit from being a peer support and 2) effectively provide academic and social support to their classmates. For example, Cushing and Kennedy (1997) found that peers who were at risk for school failure actually improved their academic standing as a result of their involvement in peer support arrangements. Similarly, Kennedy, Cushing, Carter, and Clark (2008) found that students with severe disabilities demonstrated similar academic and social gains regardless of the academic standing of the peers with whom they were paired.

Students with Limited Previous Experience

Research indicates students who typically volunteer to participate in peer-mediated interventions may differ in several ways from their classmates who decide not to volunteer (Carter et al., 2001). For example, students with already highly positive attitudes toward their classmates with disabilities tend to volunteer for such programs, whereas students with attitudes that are less accepting may not. Moreover, students who volunteer typically have had a history of spending time with people with disabilities—perhaps a close relative or neighbor—outside of school. Involving such students as peers is extremely beneficial. However, if one intent of peer support interventions is to improve the attitudes of participating students toward their classmates with disabilities, educators may need to do more to reach those students who might have the most to gain from serving in these roles.

Students with Disabilities

Students with disabilities can also be excellent providers of support to their peers. Unfortunately, they are predominantly the recipients—rather than the providers—of support and rarely have opportunities to help others (Miller, Schleien, & Bedini, 2003). Students with disabilities should be offered opportunities to provide support in those areas that align with their personal strengths and interests. For example, a student may excel on the computer, have a talent for art, or know a particular aspect of history extremely well. Educators should think creatively about how they might provide opportunities for *all* students to provide support to their classmates. In addition, several studies have shown that students with high-incidence disabilities—such as learning disabilities or emotional and behavioral disorders—can be taught to provide support to their peers with more significant disabilities (e.g., Maheady, Harper, & Mallette, 2001; Marchand-Martella & Martella, 1993).

STRATEGIES FOR IDENTIFYING PEERS

After carefully considering which students to involve in peer support activities, educators can begin the task of inviting students. Whatever approach is used, these strategies should *never* stigmatize or draw undue attention to students. One of the best ways to avoid this risk is by actively involving students with disabilities in determining strategies for identifying their own supports, to the greatest extent possible. There is no single ideal way for inviting students— each approach has benefits and drawbacks (see Table 4.1). To illustrate each of these approaches, we refer back to Yvonne, whose vignette opened this chapter. Her teachers soon recognized her social isolation and began considering ways peers might become more involved in providing support.

Table 4.1. Advantages and drawbacks of various peer support recruitment strategies

Strategy	Advantages	Potential drawbacks
Student-identified peers	Only preferred peers are chosen. Students' involvement in their own educational programming is enhanced.	Student may select peers who would not provide support effectively. Student may overlook peers who would make great supports.
Class announcements	Peers may emerge whom teachers and students may not otherwise have considered. Everyone is invited to serve as a peer support.	Initially hesitant students may be reluctant to volunteer. It is possible that no one may volunteer. Undue attention may be called to the student with disabilities.
Teacher recommendations	Teachers may have better insight into students who would make effective support providers. Identifying peers can be done discreetly.	Teacher-selected peers may not reflect students' preferences. Teacher-selected peers may not have an interest in becoming involved.
Circle of friends	A modified circle of friends approach can be used to identify a network of peers interested in providing support.	A circle of friends activity is difficult to do discreetly. Some class time is required for implementation.
Rotating peer supports	Students get to know more of their classmates. Multiple students have opportunities to give and receive support. Less effective peer pairings are only temporary.	Frequent rotation of peers may limit opportunities for friendship development. Highly effective peer support pairings are only temporary. Long-term support by the same student is precluded.
Universal peer supports	Universal approach avoids having certain students stand out as a result of receiving supports. Everyone has an opportunity to provide and receive support.	Additional expenditures of time are required. Some students may not need or benefit from peer supports or may not be skilled at providing support.
Peers from other environments	Students are not responsible for keeping up with their own work. The number of potential peer supports is expanded.	Such students may be less familiar with the course content, teacher expectations, and classroom routines. Students must have flexibility in their courses of study. Students may lack social connections within the setting in which they are providing support.

Student-Identified Peers

Students with disabilities can be asked to identify one or more peers whom they would be interested in getting to know better and working with on a regular basis (e.g., daily, weekly, periodically). As students with disabilities make the transition to adulthood, they should assume increasing responsibility for identifying from whom and how they would like to receive support. How do you determine which students they would prefer to work with? Ask them. For example, each of Yvonne's general education teachers asked Yvonne to name two or three students in each class from whom she would enjoy receiving help in the context of a peer support arrangement. In English, Yvonne quickly named Tenecia. She also identified Sonja and Marissa. The teachers could then select among those names the students whom they feel would provide support most effectively. Of course, decisions to participate must be mutual among all students.

Class Announcements

A second approach is to provide all students enrolled in a given classroom or school activity with general information about the need for peer supports and then ask students to nominate themselves (i.e., volunteer) if they are interested in participating. A class announcement could be made generally describing participants' roles and stating that anyone who is interested in finding out more about this role can ask the teacher after class. This approach is akin to self-nomination and is one of the most direct ways to ensure that you are involving peers who have a genuine interest. For example, during Spanish club, the faculty sponsor announced that Yvonne had expressed an interest in attending meetings and that her involvement would be enhanced if one or two peers would be willing to provide her with occasional support and get to know her better. Although most students knew of Yvonne, they had never really considered that she might have an interest in joining the club, nor had they considered that they could play a role in helping her to do so. Later that afternoon, three students approached the club sponsor to express their interest in serving in this role.

Teacher Recommendations

Educators or paraprofessionals also can identify one or more students whom they feel exhibit the characteristics of an effective peer support or who have something unique to offer to their classmate with disabilities. For example, one teacher asked Sarah—a student who always does a good job keeping up with her own classwork and has been a willing informal support to her classmates throughout the semester—to work more frequently with Yvonne. This approach also can help ensure that students who are underrepresented or who do not traditionally participate in these interventions are provided with such an opportunity. It also allows teachers to pick students based on certain qualities that would be likely to make them a good match for the peer. However, educators should be careful to take into account the preferences of the students with disabilities who will be receiving the support.

Circle of Friends

Several variations to the "circle of friends" approach exist (Barrett & Randall, 2004; Frederickson & Turner, 2003; Miller, Cooke, et al., 2003). They typically begin by having students spend time together reflecting on the nature and importance of their own social networks. Students are then invited by a facilitator—usually a school counselor or teacher—to take an active role in helping to expand the social networks and school participation of their classmates who have few friendships or who seem to be on the fringes of the school community—usually students with disabilities. For example, the psychology teacher at Yvonne's school might facilitate a discussion among class members about the importance of relationships in the students' lives. He talked with students about the limited opportunities Yvonne has had to develop close friendships with her peers at the school. Students were then asked to brainstorm creative ways they might help Yvonne become more involved in the class and get to know other students. The students offered a number of ideas, including joining her for lunch, walking to and from classes together, inviting her to join an extracurricular club with them, or going together to an upcoming school volleyball game. Such an approach should be implemented thoughtfully, making sure not to call undue attention to the student and reinforce others' perceptions of the student as different.

Rotating Peer Supports

Over the course of the semester or school year, peer support arrangements can be rotated, with each peer working with the same classmate with disabilities for a specified period of time, such as during a particular instructional unit or throughout the duration of a 6- or 9-week grading period (Cushing et al., 1997; Kamps et al., 2002). For example, the history teacher arranged for

Yvonne to be supported by Cynthia—a student who knows everything there is to know about ancient Greece—during the first instructional unit. During the next unit, when a group project dominated class time and required students to get together after school, Yvonne worked with Shania and Tyler, two students who lived on the same street in her neighborhood. Rotating peers provides students with disabilities an opportunity to work with and get to know most of their classmates throughout the semester. It also allows multiple students to benefit from the experience of serving as a peer support. In addition, if things happen to not work out with one peer, a new peer will be paired with the student in a short period of time. However, because students often get better at providing support as they gain experience, rotating peers too frequently may limit the opportunities they have to further develop and expand their support skills. Moreover, rotating peers too often can be frustrating for students who are just beginning to develop new friendships with their classmates. Of course, if a partnership is working well, teachers do not have to feel obligated to rotate students.

Universal Peer Supports

Using a universal approach to peer supports, every student—with and without disabilities—in a classroom is paired with one or more classmate periodically or throughout the entire semester. A variety of collaborative learning techniques employ this approach, including Classwide Peer Tutoring (Greenwood et al., 2001) and Peer-Assisted Learning Strategies (McMaster et al., 2006). Peer support arrangements are implemented for everybody, and student pairings are determined by the classroom teacher. Such an approach recognizes that students often learn best from peers and can prevent specific students from standing out as a result of their receipt of support. For example, Yvonne's teacher might decide to divide all of the students in her world literature class into several smaller groups, each comprising three to four students. The students would alternate roles within the group depending on the ongoing activity and strengths of each student. Some drawbacks might include that not everyone will require peer support and that not every student will be ready to provide this support effectively. Moreover, the time required to implement such an approach may make it less ideal when a teacher's primary focus is on supporting a single student with severe disabilities.

Peers from Other Classrooms

Peers also can be identified from beyond the particular classroom, club activity, lunch period, or gym class in which a student with disability is included (Bond & Castagnera, 2006; Hughes & Carter, 2008; Villalobos, Tweit-Hull, & Wong, 2002). Schoolwide efforts can be made to identify peers using a variety of strategies, including speaking at club meetings; distributing and posting fliers; making announcements in other classes; or enlisting the nominations or suggestions of school counselors, administrators, or other school staff. The peer then attends the general education class, extracurricular event, or other school activity along with the student with disabilities. For example, Yvonne's algebra teacher recognized that Yvonne was having trouble keeping up with her classwork. In fact, so were most of the other students in the class, as well as the paraprofessional who was working one-to-one with Yvonne. The teacher decided to ask a student who had successfully passed the course the previous semester to serve as Yvonne's peer support because this student had study hall during the algebra class. The drawback of this approach was that this peer did not know the other algebra class students well. Although she did an excellent job assisting Yvonne academically, she was less successful at encouraging social relationships with other classmates. Using peers from other classrooms, however, can be effective if the peers from outside the class already know the students in the class.

A FEW OTHER CONSIDERATIONS
Determining Who Should Participate

As students express their interest in becoming a peer support—either on their own initiative or in response to your invitation—some of the following questions might arise. How do you decide from among multiple peers who are interested in participating? What if the number of interested students exceeds the current need for peer support? Begin by using the peer support criteria you initially established to determine which students should participate during a given semester. You also may decide to implement one of the following screening strategies to assist you in identifying peers.

- *Asking the student:* Involve students with disabilities in determining whom they want to work with as part of these peer support arrangements.

- *Holding student interviews:* Hold informal interviews with interested students to discern their motivations for providing peer support and to evaluate the skills and contributions they might bring to such arrangements. Table 4.2 includes example questions that might be asked of potential peers. The appendix at the end of the book contains a photocopiable blank questionnaire based on this list of questions.

- *Getting school staff recommendations:* If you are not very familiar with students who express interest in serving in peer support roles, it may be helpful to ask potential peers to obtain the recommendations from school staff who do know them well, including teachers, counselors, or administrators. Such recommendations can be brief but should specifically ask staff to evaluate the student's prospects as a peer support.

- *Requesting written applications:* When selecting peers from within the same classroom in which the student is included, an application process is not necessary. But, if drawing students from beyond this school setting, it may be helpful to require students to complete a brief application. A written application might ask students about their reasons for interest, current course schedule, involvement in school and extracurricular activities, and contact information.

Table 4.2. Potential screening questions for prospective peers

How well do you already know _____ [student with whom the peer will work]?
What interests you most about becoming a peer support?
What expectations do you have?
What have been your past experiences with your schoolmates with disabilities?
What qualities do you think make for an effective peer support?
Are there aspects of the experience you are worried about?
What do you think it takes to be an effective peer support?
What school and community activities are you involved in?
What other time commitments do you have this semester?
What experiences have you had that you feel would make you a good peer support?
What questions do you have about becoming a peer support?
Have you had similar experiences in the past?
What do you expect to gain as a result of becoming a peer support?
Have you ever received support from your classmates? Describe the experience.

Determining How Many Peers to Involve

When making decisions about which students will participate, it also is important to consider how many classmates will serve as peer supports. Educators should not only consider how many students with disabilities will benefit from having supports from peers but also the optimal number of peers for each student with disabilities (Carter, Cushing, et al., 2005; Sasso, Mundschenk, Melloy, & Casey, 1998). Having more than one peer providing support in a particular class may expand the interaction opportunities of students with disabilities, as well as increase the number of peers ensuring that the student is engaged in ongoing class activities. Involving just one peer support can also result in gaps in support when that person is absent. Thus, it may be helpful to have more than one student involved in peer support arrangements so that support is seamless and readily available. Involving too many peers, however, can be counterproductive, resulting in students interacting more with each other than with their partner with disabilities or calling undue attention to student with disabilities.

At the same time, multiple peers can be invited to support a student with severe disabilities across the school day (see Figure 4.1). For example, some students might be identified to provide academic support within various classes, whereas others would be identified to support involvement in extracurricular activities or simply to eat lunch together. Figure 4.1 displays a

Peer Support Planning Grid

Student: Yvonne   Semester: Fall

Daily schedule	Week				
	Monday	Tuesday	Wednesday	Thursday	Friday
Algebra	Tom & Alan				→
Earth Science	Alisha				→
Physical Education	None	None	None	None	None
Lunch	Tom & Sal				→
American History	Edward				→
Drama	Sal & Jack				→
English	Tenecia				→
Club: Environmental	–	–	Sal	–	Tom
Club: Psychology	–	–	Alisha	–	–
Other: Assemblies					Anne
Other:					

Figure 4.1. A Peer Support Planning Grid for Yvonne. A blank version of this form appears in the appendix at the end of this book.

sample basic planning grid that educators can use to note how a particular student with disabilities will be supported in the different classes and school activities that make up his or her school day. A blank, reproducible version of this form is included at the end of the book.

CONCLUSION

Students are the key component of peer support interventions, and their contributions are at the core of the success or failure of these intervention efforts. As such, educators should invest thoughtful consideration when deciding which students to include. To a great extent, this should involve addressing the preferences of the student who will be receiving the support, but it also involves teachers' judgment about what types of arrangements will best meet the academic and social needs of the students involved.

5

Equipping Students to Provide Academic and Social Support

Like most sophomores at Somerset High School, Maya enjoys going to football games, meeting new people, and surfing the Internet. She loves listening to music on her MP3 player and tries to see all of the latest action movies. And, she has a talent for making jewelry, which she sells online and at local craft fairs. But, she generally is not known by teachers and her classmates for any of these things. Instead, she is mostly thought of as the girl who is always working with a teacher off to the side of the classroom and who sometimes has behavioral challenges. Maya has autism, and although she attends several general education classes, she knows very few of her classmates and has limited participation in class activities. Maya's support needs are fairly intensive, so she received one-to-one support from a paraprofessional all throughout elementary and middle school. Her teachers, however, have begun to notice some unintended drawbacks. Maya depends very heavily on her paraprofessionals for almost everything and rarely takes initiative anymore. As she will be graduating from high school in a few years, her teachers believe that she should become more independent and self-determined. Because Maya has few interactions with her classmates, her parents also have expressed concern about her lack of friendships. Maya is a wonderful person, but no one has really had a chance yet to get to know her. Her teachers know of several peers who are interested in working together with Maya in some of the classes they share. What would these peers need to know to confidently assume this role? And what would Maya need to know about working together with her peers?

From the very beginning, some students appear to be "naturals" at supporting their peers with severe disabilities academically and socially in inclusive classrooms, extracurricular clubs, and other school activities. They demonstrate a knack for understanding both the readily apparent and the subtle needs of their partners; they seem to know instinctively how to foster social connections among their partners and other classmates; they comfortably assume the dynamic roles of support, friend, and classmate; and they approach their support responsibilities with enthusiasm and dedication. Most students, however, will benefit from receiving some targeted support and information as they begin their roles as peer supports. At the outset, some students may appear fairly cautious, a bit inhibited, or somewhat uncertain about interacting with or providing support to their classmates with severe disabilities (Copeland et al., 2004; Manetti, Schneider, & Siperstein, 2001; Siperstein, Norins, & Mohler, 2007). Although these students are open to having the opportunity to work with and get to know their classmates with disabilities, they want guidance from their teachers on where to begin and how to contribute meaningfully within these peer support arrangements.

It is essential that all students serving as peer supports be well equipped to provide academic and social support to their classmates with disabilities and feel comfortable and confident in their new roles (Brown, Percy, & Machalek, 2007). In this chapter, we share strategies for equipping students to assume peer support responsibilities, and we describe the information and skills students will need to make these arrangements successful. Deliberate steps should be taken to prepare students for their new support roles—efforts that are tailored to match the strengths and needs of participating students, as well as the environments in which they will participate. At the same time, it is important that students with disabilities know how and when to request or decline support from their classmates and that they be comfortable with and understand the roles of their peers providing support. The time invested in orientation and training will go a long way toward ensuring that all students—with and without disabilities—will be successful and experience a sense of accomplishment (Stenhoff & Lignugaris, 2007).

GENERAL PRINCIPLES

As you plan for how you will equip students to provide support effectively, consider the following principles to guide your training efforts.

Do Not Underestimate Youth

Adolescents often are capable of much more than adults give them credit for. The research literature is replete with studies demonstrating the considerable capacity of middle and high school students to provide various forms of support to their peers within the classroom (e.g., Carter & Hughes, 2005; Stenhoff & Lignugaris, 2007). Even in elementary school, younger students can be quite adept at helping their classmates and providing needed support (Collins, 2002). The current generation of students has grown up attending inclusive schools and classrooms, they are experienced at working collaboratively with others, they are savvy with new technologies and educational innovations, and they recognize their potential role in increasing the participation of their peers with disabilities in everyday school life. In other words, peers often have a good understanding of why inclusion is important and how they can help support it. Indeed, students' attitudes toward and willingness to get to know their classmates with disabilities have evidenced a positive shift over time (Fisher, 1999; Krajewski & Hyde, 2000; Krajewski, Hyde, & O'Keefe, 2002).

Remain Flexible

Although students will need some initial orientation to their new roles at the start of the semester and an introduction to basic support strategies, educators can be flexible with how training is provided, what information is conveyed, and the avenues through which ongoing support and additional strategies are offered as the school year progresses. Students do not have to learn everything at the outset, and much information can be provided only if specific issues arise. For example, training can often be delivered informally through sharing additional strategies as new needs emerge; modeling appropriate interactions when necessary; or periodically meeting briefly with students before or after class, at lunch, or during down time in class.

Align Training with Students' Needs

Peers are able to provide a rich and diverse array of supports to their classmates with disabilities, such as offering help with an assignment, sharing class materials, working collaboratively on a project, providing emotional support or encouragement, offering advice, making introductions to other classmates, teaching a new skill, helping to solve a problem, making plans to do something after school, or sharing a clever joke. Academic, social, emotional, instrumental, and material supports such as these can each contribute to enhanced learning, participation, belonging, and quality of life (Fryxell & Kennedy, 1995; Kennedy, Shukla, & Fryxell, 1997). Peer support arrangements, however, are *individually tailored* interventions designed to help address just *some* of the educational and social support needs of students with severe disabilities in inclusive classrooms. Thus, the training that educators provide needs only to focus on the specific roles peers will play in meeting a student's needs. Because support needs vary from student to student and class to class, peers do not need to be taught to provide every conceivable form of support. Rather, they only need to be shown the specific strategies they will need to support a specific classmate with disabilities in a specific classroom, extracurricular club, or other school activity. In other words, the goal of training efforts should not be to prepare a new cadre of adolescent special educators (i.e., "mini-teachers"). Peers do not need—and should not receive—all of the training that special educators have received. When preparing peers to give support, providing more information is not necessarily better.

Anticipate Potential Challenges and Concerns

Inevitably, students will raise questions about the roles they should and should not assume and the situations they are likely to encounter. Some peers will have little or no hesitation about assuming this new role; others may express some anxiousness or uncertainty. It is wise to consider from the outset some of the early questions and concerns students might have and to make certain that the questions are addressed during orientation activities. Some of the common questions we hear raised by peer supports in our work with schools are as follows:

- What do I do if my partner "acts out" or has behavioral challenges? Is it my role to address these issues?
- What if my partner decides he or she just does not want to work during a particular class? Am I responsible for making sure that he or she keeps up with the rest of the class?
- What do I do if I find myself falling behind in my own work? What if I ever feel overwhelmed or unable to keep up?
- What if my partner and I find we do not get along as well as we thought we would?
- Who do I go to if I have questions, need help, or have something I would like to share?

- Will my partner and I be working together for the entire semester? For the entire school year?
- Is it okay to ask my classmates to help out too, if needed?

Talk through these or other questions students might have, and brainstorm possible responses before any potential challenges might emerge. When these issues are addressed proactively, teachers usually can ease any concerns or hesitations students might have.

Structure Appropriate Peer Relationships from the Outset

Teachers interact differently with other adults than they do with students, and students interact differently with their peers than they do with teachers and other school staff. Appropriate peer relationships must be fostered right from the very beginning of these interventions. The initial ways in which you structure and facilitate peer support arrangements will influence the nature of the interactions and relationships that ulti-mately develop (Breen & Haring, 1992; Hughes, Carter, Hughes, Bradford, & Copeland, 2002). If you only teach peers to use instructional support strategies and exclusively emphasize tutorial responsibili-ties, expect to see interactions resembling those typically taking place between teach-ers and students. If you couple academic

When adults encourage indepen-dence, offer choices, and promote self-determination, peers are likely to mirror these actions.

strategies with ideas for promoting social interaction and an emphasis on increasing class mem-bership and a sense of belonging, expect to see interactions more closely resembling those between friends or classmates. Keep aware of early interactions among students so that you can steer students in the right direction, if necessary.

Model Desired Behaviors

When paraprofessionals are seen "mothering" or always providing care for students with severe disabilities (Broer, Doyle, & Giangreco, 2005), expect peers to adopt these same inclinations. When educators always do things *for* students with disabilities, provide few choices and foster dependence, peers are likely to interact with the students in similar ways. What attitudes and behaviors do you want peers to adopt? They will learn from watching adults, so it is important to be very aware of how you and your colleagues interact and work with students with disabilities. When adults encourage independence, offer choices, and promote self-determination, peers are likely to mirror these actions. When adults use age-appropriate language, model respectful inter-actions, and hold high expectations, anticipate that peers will do the same. Van der Klift and Kunc offered the reminder that "teachers remain the most powerful modeling agents in the classroom" and stated that "if interactions between the teacher and the child with the disability are respect-ful, then the other students will take their cues accordingly" (2002, p. 25).

WHO SHOULD CONTRIBUTE TO ORIENTATION AND TRAINING EFFORTS?

Who should address the initial and ongoing training needs of peers? What contributions might special educators, paraprofessionals, general educators, school counselors, or other school staff bring to these efforts? Decisions about who will contribute to orientation and training efforts will be influenced by the environments in which peer support arrangements are being established (e.g., academic classrooms, electives, physical education, extracurricular clubs, lunch), the school staff typically present within those environments, the particular students with and without disabilities who are involved, and other staff or resources available within your school. Consistent with recommended practices in the area of inclusive education, however, orientation and training efforts should represent a collaborative endeavor and reflect the input or direct involvement of multiple stakeholders (Downing, 2008; Friend & Cook, 2007; Kennedy & Horn, 2004). It is essential that teachers, paraprofessionals, and related services providers who are all working together to support the same student align their goals for and expectations of peer support arrangements. Because these school staff sometimes diverge in their instructional priorities, expectations for student behavior, intervention preferences, and support for peer-mediated strategies (Carter & Hughes, 2006; Carter & Pesko, 2008), it is important to make sure that everyone is on the same page. This does not mean, however, that each of these individuals needs to be directly involved in providing training. When deciding on the approach you will use in your school, consider some of the contributions that these various school staff members might make to getting peer support interventions launched with a strong start.

Special Educators

Special educators are one obvious choice for leading orientation and training activities. As the lead people responsible for ensuring that the educational needs of students with disabilities are addressed, special educators must be fluent with students' 1) educational goals, 2) strengths, interests, and preferences; and 3) instructional, social, and behavioral support needs. They know which modifications and adaptations work well with students, as well as particular strategies to avoid. Because peer support interventions often are established in multiple environments across a student's school day (Haring & Breen, 1992; Kennedy, Cushing, & Itkonen, 1997), these teachers' perspectives on and attention to the entire school day can help ensure that the supports the student receives across classes are coordinated, complimentary, and comprehensive. When high schools use case management instead of a co-teaching model, special educators often have more flexibility in their schedules to meet with participating peers within or outside the classroom. However, one potential drawback of a case management approach is that special educators sometimes lack familiarity and existing relationships with students without disabilities in inclusive classrooms. Moreover, when special educators do not have a regular presence in the classroom, it may be more difficult for them to observe peer support arrangements and provide any needed on-the-spot feedback.

Paraprofessionals

Paraprofessionals often are the primary means by which the inclusion of students with severe disabilities is supported in general education classrooms (Brown, Farrington, Knight, Ross & Ziegler, 1999; Giangreco & Doyle, 2007). As peer support interventions are introduced, the roles that paraprofessionals assume within these classrooms should broaden. One of their responsibilities, for example, might involve providing ongoing feedback and assistance to the students participating in these interventions. Given this supervisory role and their ongoing presence in the classroom, it may be valuable to involve paraprofessionals directly in providing the initial training to peers or—

at a minimum—to assist the special educator in providing this training. Their involvement ensures that paraprofessionals are able to 1) determine whether peers are implementing support strategies effectively and 2) provide meaningful feedback as students work together. Because they already are present in the classroom, paraprofessionals have the flexibility to work with and assist students as new needs arise. They also will be responsible for maintaining and/or troubleshooting the intervention over time. One drawback, however, is that paraprofessionals often receive few training and in-service opportunities addressing how to provide effective support to students with severe disabilities in inclusive classrooms (see Behind the Strategies on this page).

General Educators

As the lead teachers within inclusive classrooms, general educators are perhaps the most intimately familiar with the curricular standards, instructional activities, and daily objectives presented to students. General educators determine which academic, social, and other behaviors are essential to students' success within their classroom, and they deliver instruction, reinforcement, and corrective feedback to students throughout the semester (Carter, Lane, Pierson, & Stang, in press; Lane, Pierson, & Givner, 2004). Therefore, their perspectives on the focus of peer support orientation and training efforts are essential to consider. At the same time, their respon-

---

Behind the Strategies

Effective Approaches for Paraprofessional Training

Efforts to improve the quality of instruction and educational supports provided to students with severe disabilities are challenging schools to consider new ways to use paraprofessionals within inclusive classrooms. It is essential that paraprofessionals be equipped with the skills and knowledge needed to assume these new roles effectively. Yet, many paraprofessionals feel unprepared to undertake frequently assigned tasks, lack the knowledge they needed to carry out key responsibilities, or assume inappropriate support roles when working with students with disabilities (Carter, O'Rourke, Sisco, & Pelsue, in press; French, 2001; Giangreco & Broer, 2005). Unfortunately, on-the-job training remains the primary, and often only, form of training available to paraprofessionals. More concerted efforts to improve the quality of training and supervision provided to paraprofessionals are sorely needed. Although few empirical evaluations of training approaches have been conducted, the following approaches offer promise for delivering professional development opportunities to paraprofessionals:

• On-site coaching and assistance (Clark, Cushing, & Kennedy, 2004)
• Schoolwide planning and training efforts (Giangreco, Edelman, & Broer, 2003)
• Team-based training sessions (Devlin, 2005; Doyle, 2008)
• Consultative models (Carter, Sisco, Melekoglu, & Kurkowski, in press)
• Summer institutes (Giangreco, Backus, CichoskiKelly, Sherman, & Mavropoulos, 2003)

Approaches such as these should be combined within a comprehensive, multi-tiered staff development package combining strong initial orientation programs, regular supervision from teachers, clear feedback on performance, and adequate time to plan and collaborate.

sibility for teaching 25 or more students during any given class period may leave little time for direct involvement in providing training to peers during class time. At a minimum, special educators or paraprofessionals should talk with general educators about the course information, teacher expectations, and classroom routines to be communicated to peers. Even if not leading this initial training, general educators should still know what expectations are being communicated to students with disabilities and the peers with whom they are matched so that sufficient support will be provided to students throughout the semester.

Other School Staff

When peer support strategies are implemented outside of the classroom, other school staff might be a prime choice for leading orientation efforts. A club sponsor, coach, or service-learning coordinator might each take responsibility for orienting peers who will be providing support within these extracurricular activities. In some cases, school counselors or district-level program support staff might be willing to conduct orientation and training efforts for peers. Think creatively about other potential staff in your school who may have something to contribute to these training efforts.

INFORMATION AND STRATEGIES TO ADDRESS DURING ORIENTATION

What specific needs are peer support interventions designed to address? The plan you developed (see Chapter 3) should outline the contexts and activities within which peers, paraprofessionals, and other school staff will support the inclusion of students with severe disabilities. Orientation activities should focus on the information and strategies that peers will need to deliver support effectively in those contexts and activities. Because the roles peers assume will vary depending on the class in which they are enrolled (e.g., academic, elective, vocational, arts), the expectations of teachers, the curriculum being addressed, the instructional formats used, and—most important—the students whom they are supporting, orientation and training efforts should always be individualized. There are several common issues, however, that may be beneficial to address with participating students (see Table 5.1).

Table 5.1. Possible topics to address when orienting peers to their roles

Rationale for involving peers in providing support
Background and basic information about each student
Broad educational or social-related goals
The importance of maintaining confidentiality
Expectations specific to the classroom or environment
Basic support and instructional strategies
Strategies for supporting technology and communication device use
Suggestions for giving feedback and motivating students
Ideas for promoting participation in class activities
Ideas for encouraging social interaction with peers
Seeking assistance from educators or paraprofessionals
Any additional roles and responsibilities

Rationale for Peer Support Strategies

The overarching purpose of peer support arrangements should be communicated clearly to participating students. Students may not automatically understand why their involvement in supporting inclusive education is so valuable. Consider addressing some of the following questions: *Why is inclusive education so important? What roles can students play in supporting inclusion? In what ways do you anticipate that students will benefit from working together? What are the advantages of having students support each other rather than having them rely exclusively on adult-delivered supports?* The first two chapters of this book offer some answers to these questions.

Background Information About One Another

Ideally, students with disabilities and the peers with whom they are paired will already know each other well before beginning to work together. Unfortunately, many barriers in middle and high schools prevent students with and without severe disabilities from getting to know one another. Encourage students to spend time finding out about each others' interests, hobbies, talents, preferred activities, school involvement, or social networks (see also Behind the Strategies on this page). The more students know each other, the better positioned they will be to provide support to each other. This information also provides a starting point for initial conversations among students.

Behind the Strategies

Disability Awareness Activities

"Generic" disability-related information (e.g., prevalence, etiology, defining characteristics) and traditional disability awareness activities typically are unnecessary when equipping students to provide support to their classmates with disabilities. A recent meta-analysis found that disability simulations had very limited effectiveness at improving attitudes toward people with disabilities (Flower, Burns, & Bottsford-Miller, 2007). Although providing some disability information may reduce knowledge-related barriers, there remains little evidence that such efforts, by themselves, actually translate into increased interactions among students with and without disabilities (e.g., Rillotta & Nettelbeck, 2007; Staub & Hunt, 1993; Swaim & Morgan, 2001). Moreover, self-advocates with disabilities have cautioned educators that some disability awareness efforts can inadvertently reinforce negative stereotypes (Johnson, 2006).

Disability is best understood at the level of an individual person. What does Jared like to do? What talents and strengths does Thelma have? What subjects does Elian like to learn and talk about? What help does Eva need to participate meaningfully in class? It is far more important to know, for example, what supports Meral needs than what people with labels of autism generally need or the characteristics of people with specific medical diagnoses. Although enabling peers to have a basic understanding of how a disability affects (and does not affect) their partners sometimes can be valuable, the most important information peers need is practical strategies for helping support their classmates to participate socially and academically in school.

Educational Goals

Like everyone else in the classroom, students with severe disabilities should be working toward meeting learning standards aligned with the general curriculum. Peers should understand that their partners are expected to learn many of the same skills and knowledge, as well as participate in the same class experiences, as they are. Indeed, one role for peers may be to speak up and let educators know when their partner is working on activities that seem too different or disconnected from those of the rest of the class. At the same time, students with severe disabilities also are likely to be working on educational goals that vary slightly or substantially from those of their classmates—goals outlined in their IEPs. Peers should have a *general* understanding of the broad focus of those goals relevant to the classroom in which they are working together so that they can help their partner achieve those goals. For example, students may have goals related to having more interactions with peers, using their augmentative communication device, making meaningful choices, managing their own behavior, becoming a more fluent typist, keeping track of their own homework assignments, or improving their basic reading skills. Using an IEP matrix can help identify which goals are relevant for that classroom (see Chapter 3 for more information; see the appendix at the end of this book for a blank IEP Matrix form). Peers should not see an IEP or know the specific goals as they are written; they should simply understand what the primary important outcomes are for the student in that classroom. For instance, peers do not need to know that Saul's IEP goal is to "respond appropriately to peer initiations within 5 seconds while using his communication device during 75% of opportunities." But, they should know one of their roles is to encourage Saul to use his DynaVox speech-generating device more often with classmates.

Confidentiality

It is essential that peers understand the importance of respecting privacy and maintaining confidentiality. The most straightforward way to ensure that the confidentiality of a student with disabilities is maintained is to never share private information with peers. Peers should not be told students' disability diagnoses, assessment results (e.g., adaptive behavior scores, achievement test results), medical history, IEP goals, or support needs in other environments; such information is not necessary for peers to provide support effectively. Still, peers are likely to learn things about their partners they would not have otherwise known apart from their role as a peer support, such as specific skill deficits, broad instructional goals, or other areas of challenge. The area of confidentiality can be a difficult one for adolescents to navigate without guidance, and students do not necessarily understand the concept in the same way as educators. Therefore, it is important to make certain that peers understand exactly what information should and should not be shared with others. Talk to peers about what supports their partner needs using everyday language:

It is important to make certain that peers understand exactly what information should and should not be shared with others. Talk to peers about what supports their partner needs using everyday language.

- "When Brent bangs his hand on the desk, he is letting us know he is frustrated. It sometimes can be a reminder for us to give him a choice of which task to do first. He is working hard to learn other ways to let people know what he is feeling."
- "You know how you give someone a 'high-five' when something great happens? Anna expresses her excitement a different way—by rocking back and forth."
- "That is usually a sign that Sarah is feeling a little anxious."

This kind of language provides you with a way to communicate support needs accurately while still maintaining confidentiality. If you are unsure of whether a particular piece of information is appropriate to share about a student with disabilities, ask the student or talk with his or her parents. In addition, talk with peers about how they should describe their role or interactions to other classmates who may ask about what a peer support does.

Context-Specific Expectations

Peer support arrangements can be implemented across a wide range of school and community environments, including core academic classes (e.g., history, math, science), elective and related arts classes (e.g., choir, drama, physical education), extracurricular clubs and activities (e.g., debate, environmental club, homecoming committee), community-based programs (e.g., service-learning projects, job training sites), and other school activities. In each of these environments, students can encounter a unique set of routines, activities, and teacher expectations. Confer with the classroom teacher, club sponsor, or volunteer coordinator to determine whether there are any specific rules or routines that students should be aware of. Communicate these expectations to peers and their partners with disabilities. For example, you might clarify for students when they should and should not work together, as well as whether the emphasis of their arrangement is more social or academic. If multiple peers will be working together with a single student, explain how each should share these responsibilities and balance providing support. Students also should know whether they should check in with paraprofessionals or another teacher at the beginning or at the end of the class period each day.

Basic Support and Instructional Strategies

Because peers typically play a role in promoting learning and participation within inclusive classrooms, they may benefit from having a basic understanding of effective instructional strategies, such as modeling, prompting, scaffolding, graduated guidance, and corrective feedback. The extensive literature on peer tutoring and other peer-mediated interventions demonstrates that students can readily learn basic support and instructional strategies (Ginsburg-Block, Rohrbeck, & Fantuzzo, 2006; Harper & Maheady, 2007; McMaster et al., 2006). Model these basic strategies for students, providing them with opportunities to practice while receiving feedback from you (see also Behind the Strategies on p. 60).

At the same time, emphasize for peers the importance of not doing everything *for* their partner. Although peer support arrangements can help students with disabilities become less dependent on adults for their learning, care should be taken to avoid simply transferring this dependence to peers. Peers can help their partners become more independent by gradually fading back their direct assistance over time as their partners become more proficient and skilled (Gilberts et al., 2001). As a general rule, peers should provide the least amount of support necessary to enable a student to participate in class activities or ongoing interactions.

Technology and Communication Systems

Technology can play an important role in helping students with disabilities to access the general curriculum, interact socially with others, participate fully in class activities, and assume greater control over their own learning (Davis, Caros, & Carnine, 2006; Edyburn, 2000). When working with students who use AAC devices, peers may need some guidance on basic interaction etiquette, programming the devices, and encouraging their use. Other students may use word processors, spelling/grammar checkers, speech-synthesis technology, personal digital assistants, dictation systems, digital recorders, or other computer technology to assist them in their learning. Peers should understand how this technology is used, why it is important to increasing class participation, and their role in supporting its use.

As a general rule, peers should provide the least amount of support necessary to enable a student to participate in class activities or ongoing interactions.

Student Motivation and Feedback

One potential benefit of peer support arrangements is that students with disabilities can receive greater feedback promoting learning and skill acquisition. Peers, however, may need to be shown how to give feedback to their partners that is helpful and motivating rather than overly critical. Cowie and Wallace (2000) recommended that peers be taught to 1) offer positive feedback first before giving negative feedback, 2) focus their comments on behaviors rather than on the person, 3) suggest possibilities and alternatives (e.g., "I was wondering if…" or "Do you think it might…") rather than provide directives (e.g., "You should have…" or "I would have done it this way…"), and 4) use constructive feedback. Praise generally is most effective when it is specific (i.e., clearly identifies a behavior), frequent (i.e., occurs more often than redirections or reprimands), contingent (i.e., consistently follows the desired behavior), and varied (i.e., does not always use the same praise statement; Sutherland, Copeland, & Wehby, 2001). Peers should be shown how to look for—or perhaps even try to create—opportunities for their partners to be successful and receive reinforcement. For example, Maya's peers might look for ways for her to demonstrate the knowledge and skills she possesses (e.g., encouraging her to raise her hand when she knows an answer, prompting her to contribute to the group discussion when discussing a topic she knows a lot about) and to assume roles she will know how to do well (e.g., searching for information on the Internet for a group project, making choices about which design options look best for a poster).

Promotion of Class Participation

As emphasized in Chapter 3, curricular adaptations for students with severe disabilities should be made by teachers or, when appropriate, by paraprofessionals with guidance and oversight from a general or special educator. Peers are *not* intended to take over primary instructional responsibilities for their partners with disabilities. However, there are a number of simple strategies that peers can use to assist their partners to participate more fully in classroom or other instructional activities. For example, peers might paraphrase lectures;

restate directions; clarify assignments; make sure that needed materials are available; share notes; read a worksheet, chapter, quiz, or other text aloud; or program a communication device to allow a student to participate in a class discussion. Table 5.2 presents an array of academic and social support strategies peers might use while working with their classmates with disabilities.

Providing most of these informal supports is fairly straightforward; however, peers will need to be told which strategies they should use and be shown how to do so. For example, Odessa, a student with significant physical disabilities, might simply need her peer to turn pages in the textbook, start and stop her tape recorder when the teacher lectures, and write down her oral answers on the class worksheets. For Jason, who has significant cognitive disabilities, his peer might be asked to help Jason follow along in the textbook, prompt him to type key vocabulary words into his word processor, summarize briefly the main points of the lecture, and remind him to put away his materials at the end of class. When designing support plans (see Chapters 3 and 4), teachers—with input from students with disabilities—will determine which of these roles peers will and will not assume. At the same time, peers should be encouraged to be creative in brainstorming ways to help their partners participate more actively in ongoing activities.

Table 5.2. Examples of supports that peers might provide to their classmates with disabilities

Walking with them from one class to the next
Helping keep their assignments and class materials organized
Reminding them how to follow established classroom routines
Helping them to pass out class materials
Encouraging interactions with other classmates
Helping them check the accuracy of their assignments and classwork
Sharing notes or assisting them to take complete guided notes
Paraphrasing lectures or rephrasing key ideas
Prompting them to answer a question or contribute an idea during class discussion
Using manipulatives or pictorial demonstrations to clarify a key concept
Helping them self-direct their own learning and self-manage their own behavior
Writing down answers given orally or using a communication device
Offering additional examples of a concept or ideas
Demonstrating how to complete a problem
Highlighting important information in the text or on a worksheet
Reviewing course content to ensure understanding
Supporting involvement in cooperative group activities
Teaching leisure and recreational activities during non-instructional times
Helping them to "fit in" by learning accepted social norms
Motivating and encouraging them when they get frustrated
Prompting them to use their communication book
Exchanging advice related to a personal problem
Sharing class materials
Reading aloud a section of an assignment or textbook
Redirecting them when they are off-task
Inviting them to work together on a class project
Showing them important classroom "survival skills"
Reinforcing communication attempts
Explaining how to do certain aspects of an assignment

Interactions with Classmates

A primary purpose of peer support arrangements and inclusive education is to expand students' interactions, increase their friendship networks, and promote a sense of belonging and membership. Offer suggestions for how peers can encourage interactions with other classmates. For example, peers might highlight shared interests and commonalities with other classmates, invite their partners into conversations with other classmates, model for others how to interact with someone using an AAC system, invite other students to work together with them on a lab project, make introductions to new peers, or invite their partner to spend lunch together or hang out between classes. Helping peers to reflect on the importance of friendships and social relationships in their own lives can help them to understand the importance of facilitating interactions among their partners and other classmates (Barrett & Randall, 2004).

When to Seek Assistance

Both peer supports and their partners with disabilities should know who, when, and how to ask for any needed assistance. Students occasionally may encounter challenges or circumstances requiring the involvement of a paraprofessional, special educator, or general educator. Clearly delineate and describe situations in which students should seek out help from an adult. For example, peers should not be responsible for directly addressing behavioral challenges (e.g., aggression, noncompliance, self-injury); assisting with toileting, feeding, or other medical needs; documenting IEP progress; or formally adapting assignments and tests. In addition, if students ever feel overwhelmed by their responsibilities, sense that they are falling behind in their own work, or are having difficulty getting along with their partners, they should be encouraged to let a teacher know. Similarly, if students with disabilities no longer want support from peers or would prefer to work with someone else, they should be reminded it is okay to share this preference with a teacher. If a paraprofessional or special educator is not present daily in the classroom in which students are working together, students should know whom to speak with when they need help, information, or a break from the peer support arrangement. Be proactive to ensure that students have a positive experience and feel well supported in their roles. Encourage students to ask a lot of questions and to share any concerns they have before any challenges escalate.

Additional Roles and Responsibilities

Unlike other schoolwide peer-mediated approaches (Bond & Castagnera, 2003; Hughes & Carter, 2008), peers typically do not receive grades or course credit for serving in these roles. Students also are not asked to complete additional assignments, keep reflection journals, or turn in final papers. If these (or other) additional responsibilities are incorporated into the support strategies used at your school, make sure related expectations are clearly communicated with students.

Summary of Orientation Topics

Educators should have a clear understanding of the roles they want peers to assume at the conclusion of orientation activities. If you are implementing peer support arrangements for the first time in your school, draw on the topics presented in this chapter to guide you in planning your initial orientation and training efforts. As you gain experience implementing peer support strategies, refine these efforts to reflect the lessons you are learning and the needs you see evidenced by students participating in peer support arrangements.

STARTING RELATIONSHIPS OFF RIGHT

When trying to improve the social and academic outcomes of students with severe disabilities, educators must be ever careful that the support strategies they employ never exacerbate the social and academic barriers experienced by students. Some educators and advocates have expressed concerns that peer-mediated interventions such as peer support arrangements, if not implemented well, may inadvertently reinforce prevailing stereotypes of students with disabilities (Sapon-Shevin, 2000/2001; Van der Klift & Kunc, 2002; Villalobos et al., 2002). Specifically, when exclusively tutorial relationships are established—in which students without disabilities always assume the role of support provider and students with disabilities are the designated receivers of support—students with disabilities may come to be known only for their perpetual need for help. Indeed, Siperstein, Leffert, and Wenz-Gross (1997) found that even when friendships among students with and without intellectual disabilities formed naturally (i.e., without intentional adult facilitation), the relationships that developed often appeared more hierarchical than reciprocal. Like any other form of support, peer support interventions can be implemented in ways that either enhance relationships or set students further apart.

Research examining peer support interventions, however, has not reinforced these concerns. Rather, when these arrangements are thoughtfully designed and implemented, peer support interventions often yield the opposite effect. As peers get to know and interact with their classmates with disabilities, they often discover shared interests and learn how much they have in common. Peers develop higher expectations for their classmates with disabilities as they see their partners participating more fully in instructional and other class activities. When peers' roles as *social* supports are emphasized, when expected outcomes of these arrangements are clearly communicated, and when teachers and paraprofessionals are deliberate about reflecting on the interactions students have, balanced and reciprocal relationships are much more likely to emerge. Therefore, it is essential that students understand what constitutes appropriate relationships within these interventions and that adults be thoughtful about providing the right types of facilitation.

How might you foster appropriate peer relationships within these arrangements? First, the initial training provided to peers will directly influence the types of relationships that develop among students with and without disabilities. Hughes, Carter, and colleagues (2002) found that interactions among students with and without severe disabilities looked very different depending on the roles assigned to students by teachers. When peers were assigned tutorial roles, interactions tended to be predominantly instructional. When peers were not assigned tutorial roles, interactions tended to address more social-related topics. Talk with students about the differences between providing support and providing supervision, between being a friend and being the teacher, and between offering help and offering care. Elementary and early middle school students, in particular, may struggle more with navigating these distinctions. Second, identify ways of making the exchange of support more reciprocal (Ohtake, 2003). The roles of "helper" and "helped" should not remain static; rather, opportunities should be found for every student to both offer and receive support. Educators should be very deliberate about designing instructional activities that promote students' interdependence and provide students with disabilities with opportunities to share with others what they do well. Remind students that everyone needs help in some contexts and everyone has some gift, talent, or skill they can share with others. Third, ask students with severe disabilities about the types of supports they would (and would not) like to receive and from whom they would (and would not) like to receive it. A student's support and learning preferences should always be sought out. Moreover, students should be taught how to request and decline support from others (Sapon-Shevin, 1999). Fourth, watch closely to make sure the interactions among students reflect the outcomes you hoped to foster. Research suggests adolescent friendships are more likely to develop within relationships characterized by equality and reciprocity (Brown & Klute, 2003). Do the interactions taking place among your students reflect these qualities? Are these the kinds of interactions typically leading to friendships?

LOGISTICAL ISSUES AND OTHER QUESTIONS

Where Should the Initial Orientation and Training be Provided?

Although it often is helpful to meet with peers outside of class time to orient students to their roles and responsibilities, much of the information and strategies peers will need can be shared directly within the classroom in which peers will be providing support. When paraprofessionals or special educators are already present in the classroom, they can typically model appropriate support strategies without disrupting ongoing class activities. This allows peers to ask questions and receive constructive feedback in the environments in which they are expected to actually use their new skills.

Some students with severe disabilities, however, experience substantial support needs, and it may be necessary to have a more focused training time with peers. For example, a student may use complex technology, access the curriculum in different ways, or communicate using an unfamiliar communication system. When such training is needed, educators may choose to meet with peers outside of the classroom, such as before school, during lunch, or after school. If peer support interventions become an established strategy within a school and are widely used to support a number of different students with disabilities, it may be helpful to arrange a common time to meet with all of the peers to share general information about their roles and responsibilities (Hughes et al., 2001). Similarly, if one student will be receiving support from multiple peers across the school day, it can be beneficial to gather these peers together at one time to talk about common support needs and to coordinate those supports across the school day (Haring & Breen, 1992). For example, Maya might receive support from different peers in all six of her classes. These students might meet together initially to share strategies for encouraging Maya to use her communication system and to discuss how to support Maya when she is having a "tough" day. They also may coordinate schedules to arrange times for peers to hang out with Maya between classes, at lunch, and during extracurricular activities.

How Long Might This Training Last?

Some peers quickly acquire the skills needed to effectively provide support to their classmates. Other students will benefit from a little more coaching. Expect that any initial orientation and training activities might require one or two class periods. As we mentioned previously, it can be helpful initially to meet with students for a short period before or after school or during a free period to discuss general issues related to being a peer support. Time can then be spent during class modeling specific support strategies and outlining ways students can be supported to participate more fully in class activities.

Will Ongoing Training Be Needed?

Effective classrooms are dynamic learning environments in which teaching strategies, classroom activities, and instructional groupings evolve in response to students' needs (Baldwin & Keating, 2006). Educators should expect that students with disabilities and their peers may encounter new issues and challenges as the semester progresses, new curricular units are introduced, schedules and classes change, and new classroom projects and activities are begun. Regular monitoring of peer support arrangements is essential for determining the need for additional support and training (see Chapter 7). Peer support arrangements may require occasional refinement. Meeting with peers periodically allows you to introduce new strategies or reinforce those strategies shared with peers during the initial trainings. Provide students with opportunities to discuss their experiences, share their concerns, problem-solve any challenges, and talk about what they are learning from their experiences. Talk regularly with peers and students with disabilities to brainstorm solutions to challenges students have encountered and discuss ideas for trying innovative strategies.

CONCLUSION

Peer support arrangements can be an effective approach for promoting access to the general curriculum, social relationships, skill acquisition, and other promising outcomes for participating students. However, students typically require initial information and guidance to approach their support roles with confidence and enthusiasm. The time devoted to providing this orientation and training will be time well spent.

6

Implementing Peer Supports in the Classroom

Mr. Swanson was a little surprised when John's mother—Ms. Lipsky—crossed out the words "with adult support" from all of John's annual goals at the IEP meeting. As his special education teacher for the past year and a half, he knew that John, a seventh grader, had fairly extensive support needs and would not be able to achieve all of his goals independently. Then Ms. Lipsky began to write in "with support from his class-mates" at the end of almost every goal. After all, she reasoned, wouldn't other students make better conversation, lab, and group partners than a special educator or another adult? These were the kinds of supports students naturally exchanged with their classmates, anyway. Ms. Lipsky emphasized that she did not expect John to no longer need help from Mr. Swanson during class. In fact, she commended Mr. Swanson for the ways in which he and the general education teachers adapted class activities for John. She simply wanted staff to encourage John to become less dependent on adults for meeting all of his needs. She also thought it would be important for other students to finally have the opportunity to really get to know John. She had heard about peer support strategies from another parent and thought John might benefit from something similar. Although she didn't voice it aloud, Ms. Lipsky also felt that this just wouldn't happen unless it was written in John's IEP. The conversation at the IEP meeting clearly shifted in a different direction. The team began brainstorming ways peers might be more actively involved in supporting John within his classes, as well as getting to know him at lunch and during other extracurricular activities. By the end of the meeting, the focus of John's academic, social, and behavioral goals had not changed. But a broader range of people were now being considered to support John in making progress toward those goals.

The general education curriculum is rich with potential opportunities for students to access rigorous, relevant learning experiences alongside their peers with and without disabilities. At the same time, shared learning experiences within inclusive classrooms create promising contexts for students to access social supports, learn important social skills, meet new classmates, and develop lasting friendships. Since the 1990s, the field of special education has learned a great deal about promoting meaningful participation within inclusive general education classrooms (Kennedy & Horn, 2004; Ryndak & Fisher, 2003; Spooner et al., 2006). It is clear that peers play an important—and perhaps even an essential—role in supporting students with severe disabilities to participate fully in the myriad learning and social opportunities existing within every school. At the same time, the involvement of peers in promoting inclusion must be underpinned by thoughtful planning, support, and facilitation by educators, paraprofessionals, and other school staff.

This chapter focuses on supporting students with and without disabilities as they work together within the context of peer support arrangements. Once support plans are developed, peers are identified, and everyone is oriented to their roles, educators and paraprofessionals must shift their attention to supporting students as they learn together and interact with one another. Students will benefit greatly from receiving ongoing monitoring and feedback as the semester progresses. In this chapter, we 1) discuss initial steps educators and paraprofessionals can take to ensure that peer support arrangements start off on the right track, 2) describe strategies for facilitating social interactions and promoting collaborative work, and 3) provide examples of what peer support arrangements might look like in middle and high school classrooms.

GETTING STARTED

Peer support arrangements usually begin by arranging for students and the peers who are partnered with them to sit in proximity to each other. However, students and peers should still be sitting among other classmates rather than pulled to the periphery of the classroom. In other words, students with disabilities should be brought *into* the social and instructional milieu of the class instead of pulling peers *out* to the side of the classroom to work together. As with every other student in the classroom, these students should be situated in an easily accessible location so that teachers or paraprofessionals can easily check in with and provide needed assistance to the students. When students with and without disabilities first begin working together, an adult should be nearby and available to model support strategies and quietly provide feedback without distracting the class.

Educators often choose to invite multiple peers to work with students with severe disabilities, particularly within academic classes (Carter, Cushing, et al., 2005; Garrison-Harrell et al., 1997). This ensures that support is consistently available when one peer is absent from class, offers peers some flexibility in how they balance providing assistance with completing their own work, expands the number of students who have the opportunity to get to know each other, and more closely reflects the network-based nature of students' interactions during adolescence. When multiple students—usually two—are

*Students with disabilities should be brought **into** the social and instructional milieu of the class instead of pulling peers **out** to the side of the classroom to work together.*

serving as peer supports, they may all sit together with their partner at the same table or may have their desks arranged close to each other. Within such triadic arrangements, peers should be provided with some initial guidance on when and how to alternate who will provide specific supports. For example, one peer might review key science vocabulary words with her partner while the other peer finishes his worksheet from the previous day's class. During times when the teacher lectures, one peer may be responsible for sharing her notes while the other peer periodically summarizes important points. Talk with peers about the ways they should allocate time between completing their own work and supporting their partner.

Typically, an educator or paraprofessional should talk with students and peers at the beginning of each class period to make sure everyone knows what they will be working together on and how students with severe disabilities will participate in certain class activities. For example, peers might be asked to help their partner make choices at various points during a physics lab on inertia, model how to fill in guided notes during a lecture on the food pyramid, use his or her communication book to answer questions during a class debate about an upcoming election, or search for information on the Internet as part of a group project on American poets. A clear routine should be established for when, with whom, and how often students with disabilities and their peers will check in to clarify their responsibilities for the day's class. Some teachers ask the peers to talk briefly with a paraprofessional upon arriving to class; others touch base with the peers whenever the need arises.

As discussed in Chapter 5, students with and without disabilities will benefit from some basic orientation to their roles and responsibilities when they initially begin working together. During the first few weeks of the semester, paraprofessionals or educators should pay extra attention to how participating students interact with each other and the supports they exchange. Because relationships and support patterns often are established very early on in the semester, it is important to establish clear expectations from the outset and to reinforce students for meeting those expectations. In addition, educators must be intentional about ensuring participating students have the supports and feedback they need to be successful in their roles. Peers should feel confident in their responsibilities and know exactly whom to turn to whenever they need help. Similarly, students with disabilities should be comfortable with the types of supports they are receiving, as well as enjoy working with and getting to know their peers.

FACILITATING INTERACTIONS AND FADING ADULT SUPPORT

Thoughtful monitoring and regular feedback by adults are critical components of successful peer support arrangements. When peers and their partners are left entirely on their own, emerging challenges may go unaddressed and students can easily become frustrated or fall behind in their work. At the same time, when adults remain overly involved for too long, it can inadvertently stifle the very interactions and independence these interventions are designed to promote. Neither extreme represents good practice; striking the right balance between encouraging independence and providing a foundation of ongoing support is essential. As addressed in Chapter 3, adults within the classroom should together determine what roles they will assume in supporting students' access to the general curriculum and participation in peer support arrangements. In our experiences with schools, paraprofessionals—and sometimes special educators— have typically assumed responsibility for monitoring and providing feedback to participating students.

Monitoring Peer Support Arrangements

As emphasized throughout this book, peer support arrangements are not intended to eliminate the need for paraprofessionals or special educators within inclusive classrooms. Rather, the roles of these adults actually broaden as they shift from primarily working one to one with individual students to supporting a wider range of students within the classroom. At the same time, educators should continue to monitor peer support arrangements to ensure students with severe disabilities are making meaningful progress toward their IEP goals. Peers are likely to find it easy to support their partner's involvement in some class activities but more challenging to do so in others. Paraprofessionals or special educators should notice these latter situations and be ready to step in whenever additional assistance, information, redirection, or reinforcement is needed. As mentioned in Chapter 5, there also will be instructional and behavioral issues that peers should not attempt to address.

Feedback from adults can take a variety of forms. Paraprofessionals might redirect peers when they are off task or working on other assignments, might share additional ideas for involving students with disabilities in ongoing class activities, might demonstrate new ways of supporting students to use their communication systems, might brainstorm solutions to emerging challenges, or might identify alternative ways students can contribute to group work. Most important, of course, is that adults encourage students with disabilities and their peers frequently by letting them know when they are doing well. Research clearly demonstrates that praise is most effective when it is delivered immediately, contingently, and in ways valued by students (Alberto & Troutman, 2009).

Typically, feedback can be provided within the typical flow of most class activities. For example, as a paraprofessional circulates around the classroom, she might pause next to the students to let them know they are doing well, share an idea for approaching an activity differently, or ask if they need any help. How often should feedback be provided? When students first begin working together, feedback should be more frequent and paraprofessionals should keep a closer eye on how students work together. As students get to know each other and accrue more experience working together, the schedule of feedback and reinforcement can be thinned. Classroom teams should discuss how to provide support and feedback *as often as needed, but no more than is necessary*. Although the optimal frequency of feedback has yet to be experimentally analyzed, most research studies have involved providing some form of reinforcement or feedback approximately every 15 minutes, as well as at the end of each class period (Cushing & Kennedy, 1997; Shukla et al., 1998, 1999).

It may also be helpful to develop a checklist that paraprofessionals or other adults within the classroom can use to monitor how well various aspects of these intervention are being implemented. The checklist in Figure 6.1 can prompt paraprofessionals to look for key components as students work together (a blank version of this checklist appears in the appendix at the end of this book). For example, a paraprofessional might look over toward students every 15 minutes (e.g., about three or four times per class period) to determine whether each of these questions can be answered affirmatively. Of course, the checklist should be adapted to reflect the specific roles established for peers providing support in your classrooms. When certain expectations are not being met, the checklist can serve as a cue to provide more targeted feedback and suggestions to participating students.

When paraprofessionals are not providing direct assistance to students and peers, they should be circulating around the classroom, assisting other students, preparing materials for upcoming activities, observing instruction, collecting data, or fulfilling other responsibilities determined by the classroom teacher. When adults avoid constantly hovering over or sitting directly next to students, it reduces the likelihood that students with disabilities and peers will stand out.

Checklist for Monitoring Peer Support Arrangements

Class: _Biology_   Student: _John Lipsky_

Teacher: _Mr. Swanson, Ms. Caldwell_   Team: _Lyle and Orhan_

At various times during the class, reflect on each question and check the associated box when the answer is *yes*. If no boxes are checked for a question, use the space at the bottom of the chart to brainstorm ideas for addressing this item.

Segment of class

1	2	3	4	Reflection questions
☒	☒	☒	☒	Is the student seated next to the peer(s) with whom he or she is paired?
☒	☒	☒	☒	Does the student have the same materials as his or her classmates (e.g., worksheets, books, lab materials, writing utensils, computers)?
☒	☒	☐	☒	Are the student and his or her peers *actively engaged* in ongoing instruction?
☒	☒	☐	☒	Is the work the student is doing *closely aligned* with work expected of the rest of the class?
☒	☒	☒	☒	Are interactions among the student and his or her peers *appropriate* given the context or the types of interactions other students have?
☒	☒	☐	☒	Are students completing class activities in a timely fashion or at a reasonable pace?
☒	☐	☒	☐	Are peers restating or clarifying directions?
☒	☒	☐	☒	Are peers giving appropriate prompts and feedback to the student?
☒	☒	☐	☒	Are peers summarizing activities?
☒	☒	☒	☒	Do the student and his or her peers appear to be enjoying working together?
☒	☒	☒	☒	Are students truly working *together* (rather than simply next to each other)?
☐	☒	☐	☐	Other. _Is John using his communication device independently?_
☒	☒	☐	☒	Other. _Is John turning first to his peers for needed help, rather than to adults?_

Ideas:

Figure 6.1. John's Checklist for Monitoring Peer Support Arrangements. A blank version of this form appears in the appendix at the end of this book.

Facilitating Peer Interactions and Collaborative Work

Paraprofessionals should regularly seek ways to encourage appropriate interactions and promote collaborative work among students with and without severe disabilities. Although *every* class provides natural opportunities for students to interact with one another—whether those conversations are about ongoing instruction, homework assignments, upcoming school events, or other social topics—many of these opportunities too often are overlooked by the adults who are providing direct support (Evans & Meyer, 2001). Sometimes, it is the constant presence of a paraprofessional that stifles interactions. For example, peers may feel uncomfortable initiating social conversations when adults are present, or they may perceive that it is the paraprofessional's responsibility to assist their classmate with all academic tasks. Similarly, students with disabilities often learn to turn first to their paraprofessionals for help rather than to their peers.

Other times, paraprofessionals inadvertently adopt the role of intermediary between students. For example, peers may ask questions of the paraprofessional that really are intended for their classmate (e.g., "Would Sam like to have lunch with us?" "Does Sam like to play games?"), even when that classmate is present. As students with severe disabilities work together with their peers, there often are numerous opportunities for paraprofessionals and educators to foster additional interactions—both with the peers and with other classmates.

A variety of simple facilitation strategies exist that paraprofessionals and educators can use to increase the quantity and/or quality of interactions among students with and without severe disabilities (Causton-Theoharis & Malmgren, 2005a, 2005b; Downing, 2005a; Ghere, York-Barr, & Sommerness, 2002; Kronberg, York-Barr, & Doyle, 1996). Table 6.1 provides several examples of what these strategies might look like when implemented within the classroom. These strategies are described in further detail next.

- *Modeling ways for students to interact and work together:* Initially, peers may be uncertain of how to interact with someone who communicates in unconventional ways, such as by using communication devices, adapted sign language, or gestures. Paraprofessionals can help overcome this hesitation by demonstrating effective ways of starting, maintaining, and extending conversations, as well as showing peers how to help program or troubleshoot a particular AAC device. Similarly, peers may not always recognize how to work collaboratively during group projects with someone who experiences extensive support needs. Paraprofessionals can model ways of inviting students to participate, encouraging their contributions, and supporting their involvement.

- *Highlighting similarities among students:* Whenever conversations among peers address topics related to the interests, strengths, or experiences of their classmate with severe disabilities, paraprofessionals can call attention to those areas students share in common. Pointing out that students share the same interests in music, live in the same neighborhood, or have a friend in common can spark a new conversation or provide an entry point for students to join ongoing conversation. Friendships often begin with or are built upon the discovery of shared interests. Unfortunately, students with and without disabilities often have had few opportunities to get to know each other and may be unaware of all they have in common.

- *Teaching social interaction skills:* Some students with severe disabilities may need guidance on the best ways to request help from a peer, enter into an ongoing conversation, request a short break, refuse an offer of support, or greet their classmates. Paraprofessionals and educators can teach critical social skills, provide students with frequent opportunities to practice those skills across the school day, and prompt students when opportune times arise to use those skills with peers.

- *Interpreting behaviors:* When students lack an effective and efficient means for communicating with other students or teachers, they often turn to other avenues for expressing their needs and preferences. For example, a student might bang on the desk when bored, point to a picture in his communication book when in need of help with an assignment, tug on someone's arm when ready to leave, or use a modified sign to indicate the need to use the bathroom. Peers may not automatically recognize the communicative intent of their classmate's behaviors or may overlook the meaning of more subtle attempts to start a conversation. Paraprofessionals can help interpret these behaviors for peers, explaining what each behavior might be communicating and how best to respond (Downing, 2005a).

- *Redirecting questions and conversations:* When peers ask questions of paraprofessionals more appropriately conveyed directly to the student with disabilities, paraprofessionals should redirect those comments to that student. Similarly, some students with severe dis-

Table 6.1. Facilitation strategies used by paraprofessionals and educators

Strategy	Example statements
Modeling ways for students to interact and work together	"If you show Tyler where to click, he would be able to help you finish up that computer project."
	"Madeline is still learning to use her DynaVox device. If you give her a little extra time to respond, she can usually answer your questions."
	"Here is how you can help Abby program her communication device so that she can contribute to the group presentation."
Highlighting similarities among students	"You also like country music? I think Todd went to a Toby Keith concert last week. You should ask him about it."
	"Aren't you both taking science this semester?"
	"You know who else is a movie buff? Aiden could probably tell you who starred in that film."
Teaching social interaction skills to students	"Alan wasn't looking when you said that. So, I don't think he heard you. You could ask again, but this time make sure he knows you are talking to him."
	"Can you think of how you could ask Sean if you can work with him on this project?"
	"Let's practice what you can say when you no longer want to work with a partner."
Interpreting behaviors	"That is usually a sign Sarah is feeling a little anxious. The best way to respond is usually to let her know what activity is coming up next."
	"You know how you give someone a 'high five' when something goes really well? Anna expresses her excitement in a different way—usually by rocking back and forth."
	"Bryant has a difficult time letting people know when he is getting frustrated. Encourage him to use his communication book to ask for a break when he seems upset."
Redirecting questions and conversations to other students	"Mark can definitely answer that question better than I can. Go ahead and ask him."
	"Ask your group members what they think about your idea. They can help you finish up this worksheet."
	"Anita might be willing to check to see if your answers are correct. Go ahead and ask her."
	"Hmmm...I'm not sure what you should do next. Why don't you see if Yun knows what the next assignment is?"
Identifying and reinforcing students' strengths	"It looks like everyone played an important role in getting this project done. Ruben's cover art looks fantastic, and the materials Devin gathered go perfect with it!"
	"That presentation was fantastic. You both work really well together. Looks like your creativity is a nice complement to Hayden's comic timing."
Assigning responsibilities that encourage interaction	"Amanda, can you and Robyn collate these worksheets and pass them out to the class?"
	"Evan, you are responsible for making sure everyone in your group is sharing ideas for the project. If someone is being too quiet or has not had the chance to speak, you can call on them to share an idea."
Increasing physical and social proximity	"Brian, why don't you go and sit with your lab group?"
	"Hmm...the group has already started working on the assignment and you are still way over here."
	"Is everyone close enough to be involved?"
	"Hey, guys, I think you are missing someone..."
Asking peers to provide support	"Mary, will you please help Brian with his worksheet? If you point to and read the question, he can keep his place and answer."
	"Would you be willing to be Allen's partner and read out loud to him?"

Sources: Causton-Theoharis and Malmgren (2005a, 2005b); Downing (2005a); Ghere, York-Barr, and Sommerness (2002); Kronberg, York-Barr, and Doyle (1996).

abilities have become accustomed to turning first to their paraprofessional for needed information, materials, or assistance. Paraprofessionals should encourage students to rely more heavily on their classmates for needed support.

- *Identifying and reinforcing students' strengths:* Peers may not always recognize the strengths and talents their classmates with severe disabilities bring to the class and to their relationships. Too often, students with disabilities are viewed in terms of what they cannot do. Paraprofessionals should periodically highlight those areas of strengths and call attention to the contributions students are making to group and other class activities. Increasing peers' recognition of their classmates' skills and competence may play a role in encouraging more peer interactions (Siperstein, Parker, et al., 2007).

- *Assigning responsibilities and activities that encourage interaction:* One way to highlight—as well as draw out—students' strengths is to find avenues through which students can engage in shared, interactive activities with other classmates (Causton-Theoharis & Malmgren, 2005a). Small-group assignments and other cooperative projects represent obvious avenues for furthering these opportunities. However, paraprofessionals and teachers can explore additional avenues for promoting shared activities, such as by asking two students to work together to pass out lab materials, collect homework assignments, keep track of points during practice quiz bowls or test reviews, operate the computer or video equipment when needed during class, or go to the library to look up materials related to their classwork.

- *Increasing physical and social proximity:* Students cannot interact with each other if they are not present in the same place. When students are always seated at the edges of the classroom, are frequently pulled to a corner desk for supplemental instruction, regularly run errands around the school with the paraprofessional, or consistently leave the classroom before the end of the period, they miss out on important social and instructional opportunities. Like everyone else in the classroom, students with severe disabilities should remain in the classroom and working with their peers for the duration of the class.

Although social facilitation strategies are can be implemented fairly simply by teachers and paraprofessionals, such strategies can still have a noticeable impact on the occurrence of interactions among students (see Behind the Strategies on p. 77). Of course, it also is essential that students with disabilities have a reliable and effective means for interacting with their peers. In addition to promoting interaction opportunities, educators must ensure students are equipped with communication skills allowing them to access those opportunities in meaningful ways. Table 6.2 displays a series of reflection questions that educators and paraprofessionals can pose to determine whether students possess the skills and opportunities they need to participate fully in interactions with their classmates. (These questions appear in the appendix at the end of this book as a worksheet that educators can use for discussion and planning purposes.) Additional instruction or technology should be introduced to target areas of identified need.

Too often, students with disabilities are viewed in terms of what they cannot do. Paraprofessionals should periodically highlight those areas of strengths and call attention to the contributions students are making.

Table 6.2. Reflection questions addressing students' opportunities for communication

Does the student have a means to initiate an interaction? How?

Does the student have opportunities to initiate an interaction? When? With whom?

Do others in the environment understand and respond to the student?

Does the student have a means to engage in different functions of communication, or does he or she primarily make requests or protests?

Does the student have things to talk about? What are they?

Does the student have the means to respond to others and maintain conversation? How?

Does the student have a way to correct a communication breakdown? How?

From Downing, J.E. (2005b). *Teaching communication skills to students with severe disabilities* (2nd ed., p. 33). Baltimore: Paul H. Brookes Publishing Co.; reprinted by permission.

Providing Just Enough Support

Although paraprofessionals and special educators will continue to assume primary responsibility for ensuring that the educational needs of students with severe disabilities are being met within the classroom, this should not be interpreted to mean that every support provided to students must come directly from these adults. In fact, adults should strive to increase students' independence, as well as their interdependence with peers (Kennedy, 2001). In other words, natural supports already available within the classroom (e.g., peer supports, other classmates, general educator, technologies, self-management strategies) should be considered first before introducing additional support directly from paraprofessionals and other adults. Navigating the right balance between providing enough support to promote successful participation and meaningful interactions, but not too much to contribute to overreliance, can be challenging at first. But, encouraging this type of independence is important for several reasons. First, the suppressive effect of adult proximity on interactions among students with and without disabilities has been well-documented in the literature (Carter, Sisco, Brown, et al., in press; Conroy et al., 2004; Giangreco, Edelman, Luiselli, & MacFarland, 1997; Marks et al., 1999). When a paraprofessional is always sitting next to a student with disabilities, accompanies him or her everywhere in the classroom, walks with the student to every class, and regularly pulls him or her off to the side of the class-

Behind the Strategies

Facilitating Social Interaction

Causton-Theoharis and Malmgren (2005b) conducted a research study in which they provided in-service training on basic social facilitation strategies to four paraprofessionals who were supporting students with severe disabilities in inclusive elementary classrooms. All four paraprofessionals were able to implement the facilitation strategies fairly readily and, as a result, students with severe disabilities interacted with their classmates without disabilities almost 25 times more frequently than prior to the training. When paraprofessionals and educators are intentional about looking for or creating interaction opportunities, the social benefits can be quite pronounced.

room to work on class assignments, other peers may be reluctant—or find it impossible—to work with and get to know that student. As students get older, the potential stigma associated with always having an adult present at their side only intensifies. Second, teaching students with disabilities to seek out and rely on support provided by someone other than the teacher communicates—both to students themselves and their peers—that teachers hold high expectations. Research suggests a strong link between teacher expectations and student achievement (Jussim, Smith, Madon, & Palumbo, 1998). Third, reducing students' dependence on adults to prompt and reinforce appropriate behavior can enhance self-determination (Wehmeyer et al., 2007).

Paraprofessionals often assume that if they are not always working directly with the students with severe disabilities to whom they have been "assigned," they are not adequately performing their job. Indeed, this is a primary message often communicated when paraprofessionals are individually assigned to provide one-to-one support to a particular student. Rather than beginning with the assumption that paraprofessionals should always constitute the first line of support, adults should consider how class participation might first be supported in other ways. Table 6.3 includes a series of questions educators should reflect on as they consider the ways in which students will participate in various instructional activities within inclusive classrooms. Too often, educators default to the bottom of this series of questions, providing extensive one-to-one support without considering whether students could participate in the activity with less intrusive supports and assistance. For example, rather than having a paraprofessional help a student complete a genealogy project, consider first whether the student could do it 1) on his or her own, 2) if provided with family tree software and given an adaptive keyboard and mouse, 3) if shown how to access an extensive genealogy web site online, 4) if given a checklist (task analysis) of tasks to complete for the project, 5) if provided help from peers, or 6) if allowed to work with other classmates as part of a small group. Adult support often need only be introduced when other supports are not available or accessible.

Fading Direct Support

For most students with severe disabilities, working with peers will be a new experience. Although these students are likely to always need support, this does not mean such support always has to be provided by an adult. Paraprofessionals and special educators should look for ways to begin fading back that support. Support can be reduced over time in a variety of ways. For example, the frequency with which direct support is provided to students might gradually be reduced over time. Whereas paraprofessionals might work directly with students more often early in the semester, that direct support would be thinned over time as students become more comfortable working with their peers. By the middle of the semester, paraprofessionals may only be providing intermittent assistance to students. The intensity of supports can also be reduced over time. When learning some new skills, students with severe disabilities may initially require more intensive assistance—such as physical guidance—from their teachers. Over time, less intrusive supports should be introduced, such as modeling and verbal prompts.

PEER SUPPORT EXAMPLES

What does it look like when students with and without severe disabilities are working together within inclusive classrooms? We have included vignettes and examples throughout this book illustrating the myriad ways students might work together and support one another within peer

Table 6.3. Providing just enough support

Can the student do it...
 ...on his or her own?
 ...if given the right technology or adaptive equipment?
 ...if provided with some additional skill instruction?
 ...if shown how to use basic self-management strategies?
 ...with help from his or her peer support?
 ...with help from another classmate?
 ...with help from someone else in the environment?
 ...with *occasional* help from a paraprofessional or a special educator?
 ...with *ongoing* help from a paraprofessional or a special educator?

support arrangements. We conclude this chapter with two additional examples of how peer support arrangements can help promote access to the general curriculum and social interactions for their classmates with disabilities (Cushing, Clark, Carter, & Kennedy, 2003).

Roberts Middle School

Although inclusion and equity are central to the mission of Roberts Middle School, students with severe disabilities have not always participated fully in the life of this school. As part of their school improvement plan, administrators and educators committed to rethinking the avenues through which they supported general education participation for students with extensive support needs. In addition to emphasizing collaborative teaming and differentiated instruction within professional development trainings, the school also decided to infuse peer support strategies more prominently into their service delivery model.

Eli is a seventh grader who loves being a student at Roberts. He enjoys most of his classes (except math), gets along well with his teachers (except Ms. Carver), and looks forward to going to school each day (except when he has a test). Although he has a severe disability, he is pretty typical of most students at his middle school. Rather than communicating verbally, Eli uses an augmentative communication device to interact with others, express his needs and wants, and participate in class activities. And because of his cerebral palsy, he uses a motorized wheelchair to navigate the school campus.

Last year, Eli received direct support from Ms. Shodren—a paraprofessional who is working toward obtaining her certification as a special educator—in most of his classes. Although Ms. Shodren continues to be present in many his classes, Eli now works with several peers throughout the school day. His teachers used a variety of approaches to identify interested peers, and now Eli is paired with Saundra in English, Terry in social studies, and Matthew in science. Ms. Shodren spent time with each of these peers at the beginning of the semester to show them how to use basic instructional strategies, help Eli participate in group activities, program his communication device, and encourage interactions with other classmates. As these peers became more confident in their ability to support Eli academically and socially, Ms. Shodren shifted to a more supervisory role in which she checked on them periodically throughout each class period, made sure they stayed on task, and provided any needed assistance the classroom teacher was not able to provide. Saundra, Terry, and Matthew all know that Ms. Shodren and the classroom teacher remain available to assist them if they need help or if they need to spend more time completing their own work. Ms. Shodren continues to provide support to Eli and his peers, helping Eli to access the curriculum in meaningful and successful ways. She communicates regularly with the general and special educator to make sure that the necessary adaptations and modifications are considered in advance. When she is not working directly with Eli and his peers, Ms. Shodren typically circulates around the classroom, providing help to other students who need extra support.

Eli's peers have made a great difference in his day-to-day life. In English, for example, Saundra assumes a variety of roles, including helping Eli take basic notes, learn key vocabulary words related to the lesson, keep track of his homework assignments, and record his answers. She also models for other classmates how to interact with someone who uses an augmentative communication device. Although students were curious about his device, they were initially hesitant to start a conversation with Eli—nervous that they might say the wrong thing or touch the wrong button. Seeing Saundra converse with Eli helped his classmates feel at ease. When Eli is frustrated, needs help, or wants to share something, Saundra encourages him to use his device to communicate his needs, rather than screaming. When the bell rings, Saundra and her friends usually walk with Eli to his science class, introducing him to other students they see, talking about what each plans to do after school, and helping him navigate the crowded hallways.

Eli interacts with many more of his peers than he did last year. Through these relationships, Eli is acquiring important social skills and expanding his friendship network. Instead of engaging in challenging behavior, he is learning to communicate his needs in more socially appropriate ways. Eli's peers feel comfortable letting him know when his behavior is just "not cool," just as they do with their other friends. Although Ms. Shodren has been trying to communicate this same message, Eli seems to respond much better to when he hears it from his peers. Saundra, Terry, and Matthew all try to encourage their classmates to get to know and help Eli during class. Gradually, other students are beginning to hang out with Eli at lunch and after school and new relationships are forming. Eli finally feels like he truly belongs in his classes.

The benefits of peer support interventions are certainly not limited just to Eli. His peers are learning valuable lessons, gaining important skills, and developing new friendships. Saundra, Terry, and Matthew—as well as their classmates—now have an opportunity to get to know one of their classmates with whom they had previously had limited interactions. And they are discovering that although Eli may do some things differently, he shares far more in common with other seventh graders than they had first realized. Although Saundra's parents were initially hesitant she might fall behind in her work, Saundra continues to maintain an A average in all of her classes. Matthew and Terry, however, actually increased their grades when working with Eli. Both previously struggled in most their classes, but each found the extra help they received from Ms. Shodren and the strategies they learned to support Eli helped keep them more engaged and focused during class.

Edgehill High School

Biology was easily one of most popular courses at Edgehill High School. Ms. Stiller was a creative teacher who believed strongly in engaging students and helping them see the relevance of science to their everyday lives. Hands-on labs, cooperative group work, interactive web-based activities, and interesting video clips all would be woven together to promote active learning among students. Indeed, students could often be overheard talking about the interesting things they are learning in this class. It was no surprise, therefore, that Mr. Malter thought biology would be a perfect class for Qiang to take.

Although Qiang was now a sophomore at Edgehill High School, so far he had taken few general education academic classes at his school. His previous special education teacher had difficulty recognizing how someone with severe disabilities could benefit from enrolling in these classes, so, apart from gym and art, most of Qiang's day was spent in special education classes. Although he enjoyed computers, watching sports, and music—interests shared by many other students at Edgehill—he had few friends outside of his special education classes. Mr. Malter thought biology would offer Qiang opportunities to both access an interesting, relevant curriculum and to meet other students at his school.

Mr. Malter and Ms. Stiller met to discuss the supports Qiang would need to participate meaningfully in the class. Although working in small groups was a common practice in the biology class, both teachers believed it would be important to identify a couple of peers who would be more intentionally involved in supporting Qiang. Simone and Fong—two students who shared Qiang's passion for sports and interest in computers—agreed to serve in peer support roles. Because Qiang used assistive technology, Mr. Malter met with both students over lunch to talk about how to support Qiang in using his computer more fluently and consistently. He also shared some initial ideas for how they might help Qiang get to know his other classmates, make choices, and use his communication device—all goals included on Qiang's IEP.

At the beginning of each class period, Simone sometimes helps Qiang pass out lab instructions or pick up homework assignments, which provides Qiang with opportunities to meet the rest of the class. Simone programs two or three clever comments into Qiang's communication device relevant to the materials that Quiang is gathering or that relate to some current event. When the bell rings, Fong usually helps Qiang get out all of his materials and boot up his laptop. Whenever there is down time, both peers will ask Qiang about his day or talk about upcoming school events.

When Ms. Stiller lectures—which she does sparingly—Simone and Fong periodically lean over to summarize key points or make connections to Qiang's interests and experiences to help him follow along. They also encourage—maybe even pester—Qiang to answer questions they are sure he knows the answer to. Because Ms. Stiller provides guided notes for all students, Simone, Fong, and Qiang all check their answers against one another's to make sure that they are all on the same page.

During small-group and lab activities, Qiang's peers and other group members look for ways he can contribute to the activity, even if only partially. For example, the group asks Qiang to help make decisions about which materials they should use, how they will complete the assignment, and which group members will assume which roles. When each group reports their findings back to the class, they ask Qiang if he wants to share the group's answers using his communication device. During especially difficult labs, Ms. Stiller programs hints into Qiang's communication device, and all of Qiang's classmates know they have to go to Qiang if they need help, typically making him the most important person in the classroom.

Independent seatwork, however, is the most challenging instructional format for Qiang. Sometimes, Simone or Fong will complete their work right along with Qiang; other times, they will help him after they finish their own work. Mr. Malter adapts these class activities and will occasionally work directly with Qiang to help him complete his assignments. When Ms. Stiller is showing video clips or a web site as part of the unit, however, Qiang occasionally uses this time to download all of the videos or to locate all of the web sites that Ms. Stiller has on her list.

When their work is completed, Simone or Fong might help Qiang collect assignments or materials for Ms. Stiller. Or, the students sometimes talk quietly together about a new movie they have seen or last night's football game. At the bell, Qiang's peers help him shut down his computer and gather his materials. They also help him write down his homework assignment in his planner. Although Fong used to walk with Qiang halfway to his next class, Qiang has since gotten to know two other students who are enrolled in the same class, both of whom now walk with him.

CONCLUSION

Peer support arrangements offer a promising approach for supporting inclusive educational experiences for students with severe disabilities. To maximize the social and academic benefits associated with these support strategies, paraprofessionals, special educators, and general educators will need to be actively involved in monitoring students, providing feedback, and facilitating social interactions and collaborative work. When these elements are in place, students are much more likely to access learning and social opportunities that will increase their school participation, enhance their quality of life, and equip them for adulthood.

7

Evaluating
Student Progress

Assistant Principal Mr. Bauer had just completed his first observation of Tamara Ditchman since she began working as a new special education teacher at LaGrange High School. Inclusion was still somewhat in its infancy at the school, and this was the first co-taught classroom Mr. Bauer had ever observed. One aspect of the class had especially caught his attention—Shane, a student with significant disabilities, was working along with two other classmates during almost the entire class period. During Mr. Bauer's follow-up meeting with Tamara, he asked her why Shane's paraprofessional was no longer providing this support directly. Tamara explained that when she started working in the classroom earlier in the semester, Shane did not know any of his peers, few students talked with him, and he rarely used his communication device. It quickly became obvious that always having an adult with Shane not only was unnecessary but also made peers a bit reluctant to talk with Shane. She arranged for Shane to have two "peer partners" who could help encourage his communication and support his involvement in class. The paraprofessional continued to provide periodic support to Shane and his peers, but she also worked with other students in the classroom who needed assistance. Mr. Bauer, who thought this arrangement sounded like a promising idea, asked how Shane was doing in class since working with these peers. Tamara pulled out two simple line graphs, explaining not only how Shane's conversational initiations had increased fivefold over the 2 months he had worked with his peer partners, but his time on task had increased to substantially higher levels than when he was receiving support from a paraprofessional. Mr. Bauer then asked about the two peer partners, wondering whether they might be missing out on important instructional time. Tamara knew this could be a potential concern others might express, so she explained how she and her co-teacher regularly keep track of these students' homework completion, quizzes, and overall grades to make sure that they are not falling behind. She was delighted to find one of the partner's grades had actually been increasing steadily since he began working with Shane. The other student— whose previous attendance record had been fairly spotty—had not missed a day of class since he started working with Shane. Mr. Bauer was impressed, and these data Tamara shared were certainly convincing. He encouraged Tamara to continue collect-ing her data and to share some of her findings at the next faculty meeting. Mr. Bauer knew other teachers were looking for effective strategies to support inclusion within their classrooms.

When students with and without disabilities are provided with meaningful opportunities to learn together and get to know each other, a number of substantive benefits can be expected to accrue. As discussed in Chapter 2, research indicates that peer support strategies may promote increased access to the general curriculum, higher levels of academic engagement, acquisition of new social and functional skills, increases in social interaction, greater peer acceptance, expanded friendship networks, reductions in challenging behavior, and further involvement in other school and extracurricular activities (see Carter & Kennedy, 2006; Goldstein et al., 2002; Janney & Snell, 2006). Although these research findings are certainly promising, what ultimately matters is whether these support strategies are improving outcomes for *your* students in *your* school. How can educators determine if students with and without disabilities are enjoying ben-efits similar to those highlighted in the research literature?

The purpose of this chapter is to equip you with strategies for answering two questions: Are peer support interventions benefiting participating students academically, socially, and behav-iorally? Do students, teachers, and other stakeholders view these interventions favorably? If the answer to either of these questions is no, how can these interventions be tailored to increase their effectiveness and acceptability? We discuss methods and measures educators can use to determine whether peer support arrangements are indeed accomplishing the goals that they were set out to accomplish.

IMPORTANCE OF DATA-BASED DECISION MAKING

The importance of implementing evidence-based practices has risen to the forefront of recent legislative and policy initiatives. Both the No Child Left Behind Act of 2001 (PL 107-110) and the Individuals with Disabilities Education Improvement Act of 2004 (PL 108-446) repeatedly stress how essential it is that "scientifically based" instructional practices characterize the educational programs of students with and without disabilities. Although peer-mediated interventions have consistently been identified as an evidence-based practice (Carter & Hughes, 2005; Carter & Kennedy, 2006; Maheady, Harper, & Mallette, 2003; McConnell, 2002), such a designation does not mean those benefits documented in the research literature will automatically be conferred to all students. Collecting and reviewing data addressing students' progress and overall out-comes is an essential step in determining whether and how your students are being impacted by the support strategies being implemented. Consider some of the following reasons that basing educational programming decisions on data is so important.

First, data-based decision making has long been considered best practice in special educa-tion (Heward, 2003; National Council for Accreditation of Teacher Education, 2000; Wolery, Bailey, & Sugai, 1988). Indeed, the Council for Exceptional Children defined using "performance data and information from all stakeholders to make or suggest modifications in learning envi-ronments" (2003, p. 24) as a core skill competency of special educators across the grade span. Objectively and systematically documenting students' progress is essential to designing and implementing educational services and supports that meet students' individualized needs. Unfortunately, research suggests that such ongoing data collection may be infrequently conducted and/or poorly used (Farlow & Snell, 1989; Sandall, Schwartz, & Lacroix, 2004).

Second, ongoing data collection (i.e., formative evaluation) is an important part of being a reflective practitioner. Such ongoing reflection is the only way educators will understand how peer support arrangements are affecting participating students, providing information about whether these strategies should be maintained, modified, or discontinued. When accurate performance data are available, educators are more likely to avoid the dual problems of 1) continuing to use intervention strategies that are not working and/or 2) inadvertently stopping interventions that are actually having a positive impact on students. Waiting until the end of the semester or school year (i.e., summative evaluation) to determine whether students have benefited academically and socially from intervention strategies leaves no time to make any needed adjustments.

Third, ongoing data collection allows educators to pinpoint those aspects of an intervention that are going especially well and those aspects needing improvement. With such information in hand, educators are better positioned to tailor peer support strategies to optimize their effectiveness for students. For example, a special educator might discover that even though a student with severe disabilities is interacting with her peers and other classmates more frequently during science class, the student is still not making the sort of academic progress her teacher had anticipated. Or, a paraprofessional might discover that although her students are well supported within their various academic classes, they still have few interactions with their peers at lunch, between classes, and after school. In these cases, such information can help educators focus in on those aspects of the intervention likely to need further refinement.

Evaluating the impact of peer support strategies does not need to be overly time consuming or difficult. In fact, the time invested in collecting and responding to performance data may actually save time and effort in the long run.

Fourth, data on student outcomes and stakeholder perspectives can play an important role in promoting the sustainability and expansion of peer support programs. As schools increasingly are being held accountable for demonstrating the effectiveness of their educational programs and services, data documenting the impact of peer support strategies can be instrumental in gaining or maintaining the support of administrators, parents, and other teachers. Although peer support interventions do not cost money, they still require expenditures of time and effort. Therefore, it is essential that teachers have the information available to communicate clearly the benefits and impact of these intervention strategies.

AVENUES FOR GATHERING DATA

Despite these benefits, requests for educators to undertake additional data collection efforts often are met with a collective groan. Many special educators already feel overwhelmed with other paperwork, assessment, and record-keeping responsibilities (Flowers, Ahlgrim-Delzell, Browder, & Spooner, 2005; Goldstein, 2003; Mastropieri, 2001). However, evaluating the impact of peer support strategies does not need to be overly time consuming or difficult. In fact, the time invested in collecting and responding to performance data may actually save time and effort in the long run by avoiding the continued use of services and supports that simply are not working for students or are minimally effective. Moreover, enlisting the help of others—including paraprofessionals, special educators, students, and other school staff—can make the task of data collection easier and more comprehensive.

Paraprofessionals

Paraprofessionals can assist with collecting data on student progress and, in many schools, this is reported to be a commonly assigned job-related responsibility (Carter, O'Rourke, et al., in press; Study of Personnel Needs in Special Education, 2002). Paraprofessionals often work with the same students across the school day and can compile a more comprehensive picture of the impact of peer support strategies across multiple classrooms. Such informal data collection is an appropriate role for paraprofessionals to assume within inclusive classrooms (Causton-Theoharis, Giangreco, Doyle, & Vadasy, 2007; Council for Exceptional Children, 2004; Wallace, 2003). For example, Kennedy and colleagues (Kennedy, Cushing, & Itkonen, 1997; Kennedy & Itkonen, 1994) involved paraprofessionals in collecting data on the social interactions and friendship networks of middle and high school students with severe disabilities. These paraprofessionals were in the unique position to observe students across a range of different classrooms and noninstructional environments across the school day. As paraprofessionals shift away from providing direct, one-to-one support and begin assuming broader roles within inclusive classrooms, they should have greater flexibility to observe and gather data on students' academic performance, interactions with classmates, and behavior. However, to assume this role effectively, paraprofessionals should be provided with structured data collection tools and clear instructions for gathering needed data (Martella, Marchand-Martella, Miller, Young, & Macfarlane, 1995).

Special Educators

When general and special educators co-teach within inclusive classrooms, one teacher might assume primary responsibility for providing instruction while the other focuses on observing students and collecting relevant performance data; this is referred to as a *one teach–one observe* model (Friend & Cook, 2007). When special educators assume the role of observer, they can direct some of their data collection efforts toward which students and peers are actively engaged in instruction, interacting around ongoing class activities, or demonstrating targeted skills. In other schools, special educators provide direct support less frequently to students with severe disabilities and assume service coordination or consultative roles (Dover, 2005; Giangreco et al., 2004; Knackendoffel, 2005). In such situations, a special educator could schedule periodic classroom observations to monitor students' social, academic, and behavioral progress.

Peer Supports

Peer supports may also assist in collecting information about the skills and progress that their partners with disabilities are demonstrating. Indeed, the collection of basic academic performance data by other students is a common component of many peer tutoring interventions (Mortweet et al., 1999; Stenhoff & Lignugaris, 2007). For example, a peer might be asked to keep track of whether his partner brings all of her materials to class each day, independently records her homework assignments in her planner, asks for assistance with her class assignments, writes her spelling words correctly, or initiates conversations. Peers can also provide helpful insight into their partners' social skills and interactions with classmates. For example, Haring and Breen (1992) asked peers to assist in gathering data on the frequency and quality of social interactions of two high school students with severe disabilities across the school day. The information students gathered was used to both refine the social network intervention and determine whether it was achieving its intended goals. As with paraprofessionals, the roles of peers related to any information gathering should be clearly defined and educators should consider how students' capacity to reliably gather this information may differ depending on their age, assigned roles, and relationship to their partners. Of course, careful consideration should be given when deciding which type of information is and is not appropriate to ask peers to gather.

Students with Disabilities

Increasingly, students with disabilities are being expected to assume a more prominent role in their own education. One avenue for promoting student self-determination can involve equipping students to self-monitor their own classroom performance and self-evaluate their progress toward personal learning goals. A substantial body of research has demonstrated that students with severe disabilities can learn to record and assess their own academic and social behavior performance within inclusive classrooms, especially when receiving support from peers (Agran et al., 2005; Wehmeyer et al., 2007; Wehmeyer, Hughes, Agran, Garner, & Yeager, 2003). For example, Gilberts and colleagues (2001) described how peers helped teach five middle school students with severe disabilities to self-monitor the occurrence of 11 classroom survival skills, such as bringing appropriate materials to class, greeting other students, asking questions, and recording. All five students with disabilities learned to use the self-monitoring sheet with an acceptable degree of accuracy. To assume these roles, however, students with disabilities typically will need explicit instruction, frequent opportunities to practice, and regular feedback from peers or teachers (Wehmeyer & Field, 2007).

DETERMINING THE SOCIAL, ACADEMIC, AND BEHAVIORAL IMPACT OF PEER SUPPORT ARRANGEMENTS

How are peer support interventions affecting participating students with and without disabilities? To determine whether students are indeed making meaningful social, academic, and behavioral gains while participating in peer support arrangements, educators must decide 1) which outcomes are most important to examine and 2) when and how they will document these outcomes.

Classroom Observations

Yogi Berra once noted, "You can observe a lot by watching." The sentiment of this statement is certainly true. One of the most straightforward ways of learning about the impact of peer support interventions is by taking the time to watch what occurs as students work together. Educators and/or paraprofessionals should periodically conduct informal or formal classroom observations to better understand how these interventions promote desired outcomes and to determine the effectiveness of these strategies for participating students (Carter & Hughes, 2007; Kennedy, 2004). This might involve observing several days in particular classrooms (e.g., math, science, art) or by selectively sampling a variety of different settings in which students with disabilities and their peers are spending time together.

An important initial step in this process is to determine the primary focus of these observations. The outcomes of interest must first be clearly defined so that they can be reliably documented. Because broad goals such as improvements in peer relationships and learning can sometimes be difficult to operationalize, it may be helpful to consider how these social and academic outcomes have been segmented and defined in the published literature. Specific examples of social and academic measures that might make up the focus of your observations are displayed in Tables 7.1 and 7.2. Although it is entirely appropriate to adapt these measures to reflect the specific outcomes that the educational team decides are most important for particular students, it is essential that a consistent definition be referenced during classroom observations. In addition to incorporating some of these specific measures into their recording systems, educa-

Table 7.1. Examples of social outcome measures gathered through classroom observations, interviews, or rating scales

Outcome	Example definitions	Example research citations
Social interactions	One student acknowledging another using verbal or nonverbal communicative behaviors (e.g., gestures, pointing, using augmentative and alternative communication [AAC])	Carter, Cushing, Clark, and Kennedy (2005); Shukla, Kennedy, and Cushing (1998; 1999)
Conversational initiations	New comments preceded by at least 5 seconds without an interaction or reflecting a change in conversational topic	Carter, Sisco, Brown, Brickham, and Al-Khabbaz (in press)
Appropriate interactions	Interactions typical of other peers in the same setting, or responses corresponding to an initiation in meaning and tone	Haring and Breen (1992); Hughes et al. (2000)
Positive affect	Smiling, laughing, relaxed body position, making positive remarks	Hughes et al. (1998); Kennedy and Haring (1993)
Interaction quality	Overall judgment of interaction satisfaction based on students' affect, reciprocity, and topics discussed, on a scale of 1 (*low*) to 5 (*high*)	Carter, Hughes, Guth, and Copeland (2005); Carter, Cushing, et al. (2005)
Interaction partners	People with whom the student is interacting, such as peer supports, other classmates, other students with disabilities, paraprofessionals, or teachers	Foreman, Arthur-Kelly, Pascoe, and Smith (2004)
Social contacts	Interactions with peers without disabilities within the context of an activity lasting 15 minutes or longer	Kennedy and Itkonen (1994)
Peers contacted	Total number of *different* peers involved in social contacts	Fryxell and Kennedy (1995)
Social supports	Providing information, access to others, material aid, emotional support, help with decisions, or companionship	Cushing et al. (1997); Kennedy, Shukla, and Fryxell (1997); Shukla et al. (1999)
Peer proximity	Sitting directly next to or within 3 feet of a classmate	Carter, Sisco, Melekoglu, and Kurkowski (in press)
Social networks	The number of peers who are considered to be a "friend" by the student and with whom he or she has had contact in the recent past	Kennedy, Cushing, and Itkonen (1997); Kennedy and Itkonen (1994)
Class membership	Having access to valued social roles and the symbols of belonging	McSheehan, Sonnenmeier, Jorgensen, and Turner (2006)
Peer acceptance or social status	The number of classmates who identify a student as a close friend or "most liked" peer	Barrett and Randall (2004); Mu, Siegel, and Allinder (2000)

Table 7.2. Examples of academic and class participation measures used in classroom observations

Outcome	Examples/definitions	Example citations
Academic engagement	Attending to ongoing classroom activities or engaging in class-related assignments	Carter, Cushing, Clark, and Kennedy (2005); Cushing, Kennedy, Shukla, Davis, and Meyer (1997); Shukla, Kennedy, and Cushing (1998; 1999)
Curricular consistency	Active engagement in instructional activities and materials aligned with those provided to the rest of the class or appropriately modified with respect to difficulty, modality, response format, length, or materials	Carter, Cushing, et al. (2005); Carter, Sisco, Melekoglu, and Kurkowski (in press)
On-task behavior	Behavior required of the assigned activity, such as following directions given by the teachers, paying attention to a speaker, looking at class materials, and working on assigned tasks	Sutherland, Alder, and Gunter (2003); Umbreit, Lane, and Dejud (2004)
Academic responding	Providing a specific, desired response—either verbally or in writing—to academic requests, prompts, or tasks	McDonnell, Mathot-Buckner, Thorson, and Fister (2001); Sutherland et al. (2003)
Rate of correct performance	Number of correctly completed problems divided by the time required to complete the problems	Gunter and Denny (2004)
Disruptive behavior	Failing to respond to the teacher's requests, making noises, talking out of turn, being out of one's seat, or staring in a direction other than the teacher or one's work	Martini-Scully, Bray, and Kehle (2000); McDonnell et al. (2001)
Socially appropriate behavior	Attending, working on academic assignments, reading aloud, answering questions, appropriately getting the teacher's attention, and/or complying with instructions	Christensen, Young, and Marchant (2007)

tors and paraprofessionals might also consider some of the following questions as they observe students working together.

What Do Students' Social Interactions Look Like?

The extent to which students interact with their peers, as well as the nature of those interactions, is important to understand. Because social expectations and opportunities are intimately tied to the broader context, observers should not only record whether interactions are actually taking place but also consider the appropriateness of those interactions to the activities and school environments in which students are participating. In other words, conversations taking place in a literature class are likely to differ from those taking place during a computer class. Even within the very same classroom, social expectations and opportunities will differ depending on whether lecture, cooperative group, independent seatwork, or no instruction is taking place (Carter, Sisco, Melekoglu, & Kurkowski, in press). Reflect on some of the following questions: Are interactions among students and their peers exclusively about ongoing class activities, or are students and peers also talking about social topics, such as upcoming school events, after-school activities, or other students? Are interactions heavily lopsided (i.e., unbalanced), or could they be described as more reciprocal? Are students interacting at times and in ways deemed appropriate by the classroom teacher? Many different types of interactions can take place among students and students' conversations can address a wide variety of issues (Carter, Hughes, et al., 2005; Mu, Siegel, & Allinder, 2000). One additional way to gauge the appropriateness of students' interactions is to consider whether they resemble those typically had by classmates (Christensen, Young, & Marchant, 2007). Making such a "normative comparison" can be helpful in understanding whether the interactions correspond well with expectations within the immediate context.

With Whom Do These Interactions Occur?

Obviously, interactions among students with severe disabilities and their peers should increase as they begin working together. The degree to which these interactions extend to *other* classmates, however, is an additional indicator of the success of peer support interventions. Ask yourself: Are the interactions of students with disabilities limited only to the peers with whom they are partnered? Or, are conversations also taking place with additional students in the classroom, club, or other school activity? One role of peers is to facilitate and encourage interactions with other classmates who are sitting nearby, working together as part of a group project, or who already are part of the peers' social network. It may also be helpful to note whether students' interactions are occurring with a small number of peers within the classroom or whether students are getting to know more of their classmates as the semester progresses (Kennedy, Cushing, & Itkonen, 1997; Kennedy & Itkonen, 1994).

Where and When Do These Interactions Take Place?

Although peer support arrangements offer a promising approach for increasing interactions across a wide range of instructional formats and classes, there may be times and locations during which interactions remain somewhat limited (see Behind the Strategies on p. 91; Carter, Cushing, et al., 2005). Looking at when and where interactions among students are taking place can provide insight into aspects of the school day during which additional support is needed. For example, educators should also consider whether interactions among students and their peers spill over to different classes, other school locations (e.g., hallways, lunch, recess, extracurricular activities), and outside of school. In other words, are interactions occurring during times and in places when peer support arrangements were not formally established by teachers? When interactions generalize to other contexts, this is a clear indicator that students are enjoying their relationships and choose to spend more time together.

How Do Students Interact with Paraprofessionals and Teachers?

As students with severe disabilities spend more time working with their peers, the nature of the students' interactions with adults in the classroom can be expected to change (Carter, Sisco, Melekoglu, & Kurkowski, in press). Students should gradually become less reliant on paraprofessionals and special educators as their primary source of support. As you observe in the classroom, consider the following questions: Whom do students with disabilities turn to first when they are unsure about an assignment? When they need extra help with a class activity? When they forget their class materials or need extra supplies? When they have a question about an upcoming school event? When they need assistance getting to their next class? When students turn first to their peers or other classmates for help, this is a good indicator that students are becoming less reliant on adults for all of their support.

Are Students Actively Participating in Ongoing Class Activities?

Being present in a classroom does not automatically mean students are participating actively in ongoing instruction (Carter, Sisco, Brown, et al., in press; Logan & Malone, 1998). When work-

---

Behind the Strategies

Using Time Sampling to Conduct Classroom Observation

It is important for educators to use an approach to direct observation that yields reliable information without being too cumbersome (Gunter & Denny, 2004). Indeed, the perceived time and effort required to conduct classroom observations is often cited as a barrier to regular data collection in schools (Alberto & Troutman, 2009). Among the wide variety of recording systems available to teachers, interval recording may be one of the most feasible (Cooper, Heron, & Heward, 2007; Kennedy, 2005). Momentary interval recording involves dividing a class period or other observation period into equal intervals (e.g., 1 minute, 5 minutes, 10 minutes) and observing whether students are performing the targeted behaviors at the *end* of the interval. Rather than having to observe continuously, teachers observe during relatively brief, but equally spaced, observation intervals. For example, a paraprofessional might look over at a student and his or her peers every 5 minutes to record whether or not they are staying on task during class activities. This recording system is most appropriate for continuous behaviors, such as academic engagement, curricular consistency, or peer proximity. Partial interval recording also involves dividing an observation period into equal intervals, but target behaviors are instead counted if they occur at any point during the interval. For example, a special educator might record whether a student with disabilities converses with other classmates any time during each of four 15-minute intervals during biology class. This recording system is most appropriate for behaviors that are shorter in duration and/or that occur less frequently, such as social interactions, disruptive behaviors, or academic responding. Within both recording systems, using smaller time intervals generally increases the likelihood that the data gathered will more closely approximate the actual occurrence of the behavior (Gunter, Venn, Patrick, Miller, & Kelly, 2003).

---

ing with their peers, students with severe disabilities should be meaningfully engaged in challenging and relevant learning activities. At the same time, peers should be expected to keep up with their own classwork and not be hampered academically by assuming their responsibilities. As you observe, ask yourself: Are students with disabilities paying attention to lectures, contributing to class discussions, participating in group projects, completing class assignments, and participating in other assigned activities? Are they on the same page of the textbook, worksheet, class notes, or web site as their classmates? Are they assuming valued roles within typical classroom routines and activities? Although the ways students with severe disabilities engage with the curriculum may look somewhat different, educators should hold high expectations that all students will participate actively in all learning activities.

Are Materials and Activities Appropriate for Students?

Accessing the general curriculum means receiving instruction related to the same local and state content standards as other students in the classroom (Cushing et al., 2005). Although students with severe disabilities will require individually designed adaptations, modifications, and supports to ensure they can make progress toward these standards, educators should be vigilant about making certain those supports are in place. As you observe, consider the following questions: Are the course materials and activities adapted such that they are consistent with both the intended curriculum and students' IEP goals? Are students engaged with materials related to course content or activities provided by the teacher, or are they working on activities that are entirely different? Are materials being adapted "on the fly" or well in advance of introducing new instructional activities? Are adaptations age appropriate, functional, and the least intrusive possible? Although it should not be peers' responsibility to make these adaptations, peers can still alert the paraprofessional or the classroom teacher when their partners' materials and activities differ substantially from those of the rest of the class.

How Are Peer Supports Providing Assistance to Their Partners?

Peers are likely to provide a range of academic, social, and/or behavioral assistance to their partners with disabilities, as determined during initial orientation activities and periodic discussions with teachers. For example, peers may work with their partners on assignments, supporting involvement in cooperative groups, paraphrasing lectures, asking clarifying questions, reviewing work, offering corrective feedback, making sure needed materials are available, and/or explaining how to complete certain aspects of an assignment. Are peers providing these supports consistently and effectively? Are those supports being provided in ways that encourage independence, promote learning, and evidence reciprocity? Are supports provided in respectful ways that foster, rather than stifle, perceptions of competence among classmates?

Curricular Progress and Academic Learning

In addition to observing how students interact with each other and participate in ongoing class activities, it also is important to document the educational progress that students with and without disabilities are making while participating in peer support arrangements. How do you evaluate the degree to which students are benefiting academically from peer support strategies? What indicators might point to whether students are making expected progress as they work together in various classrooms? As discussed in Chapter 1, expectations related to what students with severe disabilities can and should learn have increased dramatically in recent years. Although research on effective approaches

Ask yourself: Are students with disabilities paying attention to lectures, contributing to class discussions, participating in group projects, completing class assignments, and participating in other assigned activities? Are they assuming valued roles within typical classroom routines and activities?

for documenting academic progress and learning outcomes for students with severe disabilities within the general curriculum is continuing to expand, this area of research still remains somewhat in its infancy. In addition to conducting classroom observations of academic engagement, educators might consider some of the following approaches to more directly document educational progress.

- *IEP progress:* The IEP outlines the academic and functional goals that a student with a disability is expected to accomplish and delineates how progress will be measured. Educators must regularly monitor students' performance on these goals and determine whether it is commensurate with the expectations outlined by the IEP team. As students work with their peers, they should continue to make adequate progress on those IEP goals relevant to the classroom in which students are working together (Hunt et al., 1994). Such progress should be regularly documented, not simply assumed.

- *Skill acquisition:* Educators often identify specific skills they want students to develop further while students are working with their peers. Regularly assessing whether students are indeed learning, using, and/or maintaining those skills is another way to determine the efficacy of peer support arrangements. For example, teachers might document progress on letter-writing skills in an English composition class (Collins et al., 2001); monitor motor, fitness, and recreational skill acquisition in a physical education class (Barfield, Hannigan-Downs, & Lieberman, 1998); or assess the extent to which students learn to use critical social skills within elective classes (Hughes, Copeland, et al., 2002). A variety of systematic approaches exist for gathering data on skill acquisition and are described in most introductory textbooks focused on education of students with severe disabilities (Alberto & Troutman, 2009; Snell & Brown, 2006; Westling & Fox, 2004).

- *Curriculum-based measures:* Curriculum-based measurement is an approach to progress monitoring that considers students' performance within the curriculum of a specific course. Academic performance is assessed by sampling from the entire curriculum and regularly evaluating students' mastery of that content (Deno, 2003). For example, a teacher might identify all of the sight words a student is expected to learn within the science curriculum during the year and then periodically sample a portion of those words to determine how many a student is able to read. Although widely used with students with high-incidence disabilities, application of these strategies for students with severe disabilities has lagged somewhat behind (Browder, Wallace, Snell, & Kleinert, 2005).

- *Homework and assignment completion:* Another indicator of academic progress involves monitoring the homework and/or assignment completion of both students with and without disabilities (Christensen et al., 2007; McDonnell et al., 2001). If students with disabilities or their peers are not consistently keeping up with these task responsibilities or the overall quality of their submitted work declines, the students and peers may need additional support or assistance.

- *Work samples:* Teachers often use portfolios of students' work to gauge what students know and can do (Guskey, 2007). Portfolio assessment also has emerged as a valuable strategy for documenting the academic progress of students with severe disabilities within the general curriculum (Kearns, Burdge, Clayton, Denham, & Kleinert, 2006). For example, a teacher might gather multiple samples of a student's work (e.g., homework assignments, group projects, class notes, lab activities) to examine its quality, connection to the broader curriculum, and the extent to which it evidences improvement over time. In addition, examples of students' performance within the classroom might be photographed or videotaped for inclusion in alternate assessment packages and accompanied by a description of the roles peers played in supporting that work.

- *Quizzes and tests:* Structured quizzes and tests can also serve as indicators of knowledge and skill acquisition. For students with severe disabilities, such assessments will need to be thoughtfully adapted to ensure that they reflect the instructional content students were expected to master as well as allow students to respond in ways truly reflecting their understanding of the material. At the same time, performance on classroom quizzes and tests provides another avenue for determining the academic performance of peer supports as they participate in these classroom interventions.

Additional Indicators

In addition to classroom observations and more direct measures of academic performance, several other potential outcomes might be examined when considering the impact of peer support arrangements. First, educators often mention anecdotally that students serving as peer supports—particularly those who are at risk for school failure or who are struggling to see the relevance of school to their lives—sometimes seem more motivated to attend class when they begin assuming this support role. The same might also be true for students with severe disabilities, who often look forward more to attending class and having better opportunities to interact with their classmates when they receive support from their peers. Look into whether class and school attendance patterns change for students who are involved in these arrangements. Second, as students get to know and spend more time with their peers without disabilities, their participation in a wider range of school activities should increase. Keep track of the extent to which students with severe disabilities are involved in extracurricular clubs, student organizations, and other school-sponsored events. Such increases in involvement might be due to the encouragement, support, and advocacy of peer supports or may also result from students simply having greater exposure to the range of extracurricular opportunities through conversations with their classmates.

OBTAINING FEEDBACK FROM STUDENTS, EDUCATORS, AND OTHER STAKEHOLDERS

Another element critical to the success of any school-based intervention is the extent to which students, staff, and others involved in and/or affected by that intervention are supportive of and satisfied with its goals, procedures, and outcomes. If teachers do not perceive that a particular intervention approach holds promise for improving students' educational outcomes and quality of life, is practical to implement given their current resources and other instructional priorities, is a good fit within their usual classroom routines and practices, or is valued by administrators and parents, teachers are unlikely to adopt that practice, implement it with sufficient fidelity, or maintain it over time. In the research literature, this concept often is called *social validity*. Social validity refers to the appropriateness and relevance of intervention goals, the acceptability of the specific intervention strategies used to achieve those goals, and the impact and importance of attaining those goals to the lives of students (Kennedy, 2005; Schwartz & Baer, 1991; Wolf, 1978). Put simply, social validity refers to how useful various aspects of the intervention are to key stakeholders.

Although the research literature offers strong indications that peer support arrangements are judged to be acceptable and practical intervention approaches for elementary and secondary inclusive classrooms (Carter & Kennedy, 2006; Carter & Pesko, 2008; Kamps et al., 1998), a primary concern for educators should center around whether these intervention strategies are well received and beneficial for students within *their* classrooms and schools. Here is just a sampling of the questions that might be raised when reflecting on the acceptability and impact of peer support interventions.

- Do educators, parents, administrators, and students themselves believe that improving social relationships and academic participation is an important educational goal for students with disabilities?

- Do they think that peer support strategies are an acceptable and promising approach for meeting these goals?

- Do educators and paraprofessionals find that peer support arrangements are easy or difficult to implement?

- Are students with and without disabilities enjoying working together and believe that they are benefiting personally from the involvement?

- Are paraprofessionals comfortable with and adequately prepared to assume new and broader roles within inclusive classrooms?

- Are noticeable improvements in students' social, learning, and behavioral outcomes readily apparent to others?

- Are students with disabilities assuming valued roles and responsibilities within the classroom?

- Are peer support interventions continuing to meet the needs of students and teachers as the semester progresses?

- Do administrators support expanding these intervention strategies to other classrooms or aspects of the school day?

How might you begin to answer some of these questions? A variety of approaches can be used to provide insight into the acceptability and impact of peer support interventions, including holding informal conversations with various students, school staff, and others; periodically observing classrooms and other environments in which students spend time together; distributing brief questionnaires; or examining whether peer support arrangements and peer relationships are maintained over time (Kennedy, 2002a). Because peer support interventions can affect more than just the students who are directly involved, it can be valuable to gather feedback and insights from a variety of people, including students with disabilities, peer supports, other classmates, paraprofessionals, special educators, general educators, administrators, and parents. Each of these stakeholders has a different vantage point and may hold somewhat different perspectives on the benefits, challenges, and possibilities associated with these intervention strategies.

Students with Disabilities

Historically, students with severe disabilities have been afforded limited opportunities to offer meaningful input into their own education (Wehmeyer & Sands, 1998). Increasingly, advocates, researchers, and policy makers are calling for a fundamental shift in expectations for these students, challenging schools to involve students more actively in educational planning and more directly in determining their own supports (Keefe, Moore, & Duff, 2006; Martin, Van Dycke, Greene, et al., 2006). Students—particularly adolescents—should have a say in the courses they take and the supports they receive within those classrooms. Unfortunately, research indicates

Students—particularly adolescents—should have a say in the courses they take and the supports they receive within those classrooms.

that the perspectives and feedback of students with disabilities are inconsistently considered when schools plan and evaluate service delivery approaches (Broer et al., 2005; Hemmingsson et al., 2003; Skär & Tamm, 2001).

As emphasized in previous chapters, the preferences of students with disabilities should be considered throughout efforts to design and implement peer support arrangements. How do your students with severe disabilities feel about working with peers? Do they enjoy working with their classmates in this way? Are there other students they would prefer working with? Do they feel they are benefiting from their experiences? Do they want to continue participating in these interventions? Would they like to have peer support arrangements established in their other classes or school activities? Lane and Beebe-Frankenberger pointed out that "student buy-in of an intervention is often assumed and seldom assessed" (2004, p. 97).

Educators can gather feedback from students in several ways. The obvious starting point is to simply ask students to share their thoughts on being matched with a peer and their experiences within their various classes. For example, Broer et al. (2005) interviewed young adults with intellectual disabilities about their experiences in school. These former students offered insightful comments about the supports they received and shared helpful recommendations and advice for teachers on improving classrooms. Table 7.3 includes a list of reflection questions educators can use to start such a discussion with students. These questions also appear as a worksheet (Reflection Questions for Students with Disabilities) in the appendix at the end of this book. Because students will vary in their ability to understand these questions or clearly express their perspectives, teachers should phrase questions so that they are understandable and align with students' preferred communication mode.

Sometimes, it can be challenging to discern the recommendations and preferences of students, especially when they are younger or experience substantial communicative or cognitive challenges. Observing students as they work with their peers in various classrooms offers another avenue for understanding whether students are satisfied with the supports they are receiving and their participation in class. Do students seem to be enjoying working with their peers? Are they smiling, laughing, joking, or having fun? Do they interact frequently with their peers? Do they seek out their peers when they arrive to class or at other times of day (e.g., lunch, transition times, before and after school)? Do they look forward to coming to class each day? When given the option to work with their peers, with adults (e.g., paraprofessional, special educator), or alone, what do they choose?

Table 7.3.   Reflection questions for students with disabilities

Are you enjoying spending time with _____? Why or why not?

What are some of the things you do together?

What do you find most helpful? Least helpful?

What do you like or dislike about the supports you receive?

What have you learned from working with _____?

How has _____ benefited from getting to know you?

Do you consider _____ to be a friend?

Is there any other help you think you would need in this class?

Would you like to continue working with _____? If not, why not?

Do you do things with _____ outside of school?

Are there other things you would like to do with _____ outside of the class?

Have you made other new friends in this class? Elsewhere in school?

What would you like your teachers to know about how best to support you in class?

Sources: Broer, Doyle, and Giangreco (2005); Hughes and Carter (2008); Hughes et al. (1999); Hughes et al. (2000).

Peers without Disabilities

Students without disabilities also have much to offer by way of recommendations and feedback on the acceptability and potential benefits of peer support interventions. Their active involvement in providing supports to their classmates with disabilities gives them a unique perspective on what might be working well and what additional refinements may be needed. Students also have a unique insight into the peer culture and the perceptions of other classmates at their school, holding a perspective that adults generally are not privy to or do not share. In other words, students tend to view and understand the social dynamics within the classroom and school somewhat differently than do teachers. The research literature contains numerous examples of how the feedback of students without disabilities has shaped our field's understanding of inclusion and how to do it well (e.g., Fisher, 1999; Hendrickson et al., 1996; Siperstein, Parker, et al., 2007; Williams & Downing, 1998; York & Tundidor, 1995).

Set aside time to talk with students who are serving in peer support roles about their experiences, the lessons they are learning, the benefits they have observed, and their advice for making the process more meaningful. Table 7.4 includes a variety of questions educators can use to prompt these conversations with peers; these questions are also provided as a worksheet (Reflection Questions for Peers) in the appendix at the end of this book. In addition, it may be instructive to ask students about how their involvement as a peer support is perceived by other classmates. What do those classmates say about inclusion and how do they view its importance? These questions can be asked periodically as paraprofessionals or educators check in with students during class, or separate meetings might be held over the lunch period, before or after school, or at some other mutually agreeable time. If peer support arrangements are used in mul-

Table 7.4. Reflection questions for peers

How would you describe your experience working with your partner?

Did you enjoy serving in this role? In what ways? What did you like most?

What things have been going really well? Not so well?

Were there aspects of this role you particularly enjoyed? Found difficult?

In what ways have you benefited from participating in this way? What have you learned?

How effective do you feel you are in this role? Are you comfortable with your responsibilities?

What changes have you noticed in your partner, if any?

Do you think this was a beneficial experience for your partner? If so, how?

What have you learned about the most effective ways to support your partner?

What strategies have been working really well? Not so well?

Is there any additional support or help that you feel would help you to be more effective in this role?

Would you like to continue in this role in the future? Why or why not?

Are there other things you would like to do with your partner?

What makes someone a member of this class?

How do other students in the classroom understand your role as a peer support?

Sources: Bond and Castagnera (2003); Copeland et al. (2004); Hughes et al. (2001); Jones (2007); Kamps et al. (1998); Williams and Downing (1998).

tiple classrooms throughout the school, consider arranging a common time for all of the students who are serving in peer support roles to gather together for a feedback and brainstorming session (Copeland et al., 2004; Haring & Breen, 1992). In addition to providing teachers with new insights into the impact of peer support interventions, such a gathering allows students to hear the experiences and advice of other students who also are serving in the same role.

During these conversations, pay close attention to how students speak about their interactions and relationships with their partners with disabilities. Meyer emphasized that "if children continually describe those interactions as 'working with' and 'helping' the child with disabilities, what would otherwise be normalised helping situations turn into a hierarchical social status among children" (2001, p. 18). The language students use and examples they share can help you gauge whether emerging relationships resemble those that were originally intended. Do students speak about their partners in positive, respectful, and affirming ways? Are the activities that the students say they do together appropriate, given your expectations? If not, consider what steps you might take to redirect these interactions in different directions (Hughes, Carter, et al., 2002).

In addition to talking directly with students, educators might develop a short written questionnaire asking peers to share their thoughts on several issues. This provides an efficient way to gather impressions and suggestions when many students are serving as peer supports. For example, students might be asked why they decided to become involved, how they feel they have benefited from the experience, whether they plan to continue in this role in the future, and what recommendations they have for helping their partner participate more fully in class and school. A number of questionnaires already exist and can readily be adapted to activities at your local school (Bond & Castagnera, 2003; Hughes & Carter, 2008; Jones, 2007; Longwill, 2002; Montgomery, Benito, Valdes, Magers, & Taluga, 2005; Villalobos et al., 2002). If used, these questionnaires should be brief, focused, and straightforward to complete so that they provide information useful for strengthening the quality of peer support activities at your school.

Educators and Paraprofessionals

The support of paraprofessionals, special educators, and general educators is critical to the success of any classroom intervention, and peer support arrangements are no exception. This support can be influenced by at least four factors, as illustrated in each of the following questions: Does the intervention produce noticeable improvements in student outcomes (*effectiveness*)? Is it easy enough to implement (*feasibility*)? Does it fit within existing classroom routines (*acceptability*)? Do staff feel confident in their ability to implement it properly (*training*)? These factors are not necessarily equivalently weighted. A paraprofessional might be very willing to continue using an intervention requiring significant expenditures of time and effort if he or she perceives that the benefits for students are substantial. Similarly, a classroom teacher may be open to changing his or her established instructional routines if an intervention appears to be reasonably easy to implement and promises to be effective. Find out from these school staff how they perceive the effectiveness, feasibility, and acceptability of peer support interventions, as well as whether they feel they have the training needed to implement them with fidelity. Table 7.5 includes a sampling of reflection questions that might form the basis for these discussions with these other staff. These questions are presented in worksheet format (Reflection Questions for Paraprofessionals and Educators) in the appendix at the end of this book.

Peer support interventions typically involve shifting the responsibilities paraprofessionals assume within inclusive classrooms—from a one-to-one to a broader support role—and call on

Table 7.5.   Reflection questions for paraprofessionals and educators

What has been your overall reaction to implementing peer support strategies?

How would you describe the experiences of students who are participating in these arrangements?

How effective have peers been at providing academic support to their classmates with severe disabilities? Social support?

Are there strategies that peers still need to learn that would make them more effective at supporting their classmates?

What role have peers played in contributing to an inclusive classroom or school?

What concerns do you have about implementing peer support arrangements in your classroom?

What sort of assistance would be most helpful for you?

In your opinion, what have been the benefits of peer support arrangements to students with disabilities? To their classmates without disabilities? To the peers participating in the peer support initiatives? To school staff?

What aspects of inclusion have been most challenging for you?

What additional informational, resource, or training needs do you have related to including students with severe disabilities in your classroom?

Do you have specific concerns about some aspect of peer support arrangements?

Will you continue to use peer support arrangements in this classroom in the future? How about in other classrooms?

Sources: Copeland, McCall, et al. (2002); Cushing et al. (1997); Hughes and Carter (2008); Janney, Snell, Beers, and Raynes (1995); York and Tundidor (1995).

these staff to change some often-long-established practices. Therefore, it is important to regularly ask paraprofessionals for their feedback on the extent to which they understand and feel equipped to assume these new roles. Causton-Theoharis and colleagues (2007) recommended establishing regular, designated times for special educators and paraprofessionals to meet to discuss issues related to supporting students with disabilities in various classrooms. These check-in times allow paraprofessionals to receive needed guidance and feedback from special educators, share their observations of how well students and their peers are working together, and brainstorm any adjustments that may be needed to the peer support arrangements.

The perspectives of general educators on the social validity of these interventions are especially important to consider. What academic, social, and behavioral expectations do these teachers hold for their classrooms? Because general and special educators sometimes hold divergent expectations for their classrooms (Carter & Hughes, 2006; Carter, Lane, Pierson, & Stang, in press), it is important that everyone shares the same understanding of priority goals for students with severe disabilities who are enrolled in the classroom. Ask these teachers if they think that participating students with disabilities are meeting or making progress toward these goals. What have they noticed about the ways students and their peers are working together? Are students benefiting in the ways teachers had hoped? What recommendations do they have for improving peer support arrangements or involving peers in slightly different ways? Feedback from other teachers can be gathered in a variety of ways, including informal conversations after school or over lunch, during departmental faculty meetings, during in-service days, or through e-mail.

Family Members

Parents of children and youth with severe disabilities frequently identify promoting friendships and school inclusion as a valued outcome (Overton & Rausch, 2002; Palmer, Fuller, Arora, & Nelson, 2001). Their perspectives on the role of peer support strategies in promoting these outcomes should be sought during the educational planning process, as well as revisited periodically as the school year progresses. Parents can share unique insight into how their child talks about their school day and describes their relationships with their peers and other classmates, as well as share whether their child is getting together with, talking to, or communicating electronically (e.g., e-mail, instant messaging, social networking, webcams) with their peers or other classmates outside of the school day. Periodically ask for feedback from parents about what they notice or hear at home about their child's experiences during the school day and how they perceive that their child might be benefiting from the intervention. Asking parents of participating peers to share their insights might also help educators better understand the broader impact of these interventions. For example, Peck, Staub, Gallucci, and Schwartz (2004) asked parents of elementary students without disabilities to share how their children benefited socially and academically from participating in inclusive classrooms. Parents were overwhelmingly positive, and their feedback contributed new insights into how educational services and supports might be strengthened within these classrooms.

CONCLUSION

Being an effective practitioner requires gathering sound data on student performance and the broader impact of intervention efforts, reflecting carefully on those findings, and adjusting instructional programs and supports accordingly. Such a data-driven approach can assist you in addressing potential challenges before they emerge, tailoring interventions to better meet the needs of individual students, identifying benefits that might not be readily apparent, and adapting peer support activities in response to feedback and recommendations from students and other stakeholders. What if peer support strategies are not having the desired impact you initially had anticipated? Be flexible and willing to adjust the ways in which students work together until you discover the right fit. A consistent finding in the research literature is that when educators implement peer support strategies in their classrooms, they can expect to see substantial benefits. It is essential, however, that deliberate efforts be made to document these outcomes and adjust support strategies in response.

8

Epilogue

How Far Can We Go?

In the initial chapter of this book, we address the question, "How far can we go?" As noted from an historical context, peer support interventions have emerged as a significant element in the inclusive education of students with severe disabilities. Peer support interventions have been designed to facilitate social relationship development among peers with and without disabilities in contexts where social interactions are often limited. In addition, there is evidence that academic benefits accrue for both students with and without disabilities. On top of these student benefits, peer support interventions increase resources for general and special educators by allowing paraprofessionals and other adults to serve in support roles for an entire general education class rather than for a single student.

In this final chapter of the book, we would like to pose a few questions that reflect on the question, "How far can we go?" Because many advances have been made in peer support interventions, it seems appropriate to consider what directions new advances may take. Just like monitoring student progress and noting when and where student outcomes are improving leads to a new series of instructional objectives, this chapter seems an appropriate place to consider what the next steps for peer supports might be.

WHAT NEW OPPORTUNITIES CAN BE DEVELOPED THROUGH PEER SUPPORTS?

Our current knowledge of peer supports has focused primarily on general education classrooms. This makes a great deal of sense because the initial impetus for developing peer supports was to gain social and academic benefits from including students with severe disabilities into general education classes. In fact, most research on peer support interventions has focused on academic-oriented learning environments such as English/language arts, math, science, and social studies. This leaves a large range of school contexts, however, that have yet to receive research attention regarding support strategies and student outcomes.

An obvious direction is to more systematically extend peer support strategies to—for the lack of a better term—"nonacademic" classes such as art, music, physical education, and so forth. The interventions discussed in this book were developed for classroom environments where student-to-student interaction has traditionally been minimized (and often "punished" by referrals to the assistant principal's office). We and others have begun to extend peer support strategies to a broader range of school classes, but this work is still in its early stages. And, as with all educational interventions, peer support procedures will need to be adapted to best fit these environments. Issues to be addressed might include incorporating peer support arrangements into a larger and less defined social milieu, defining appropriate roles for paraprofessionals in educational environments where only one adult is typically present, and making peer-delivered curricular modifications/adaptations appropriate for these new contexts.

Similarly, it will be interesting to see how peer support interventions are adapted to meet the needs of students within extracurricular settings. Contexts such as dances, school newspapers, sporting events, thematic clubs, service-learning projects, and student governance all provide potentially rich places to meet others, develop relationships, and learn new skills. However, it remains unclear how peer support strategies will be adapted to these important, but understudied, social situations.

Within all of these contexts, there are a set of issues that need to be addressed because they are fundamental to the success of all educational interventions, and we have learned through a great deal of experience that if these issues are not explicitly addressed, valued outcomes will only sporadically occur. That is, how will peer support interventions be engineered so that they produce generalized social and academic benefits, are sustained over time, and withstand varying degrees of intervention fidelity? Each of these is a significant issue that intertwines social validity, measurable outcomes, operationalized procedures, and replicable results. It is likely that the next generation of peer support research will address these questions in ways that are more integrative than previous efforts made with less contextually dependent interventions. If these efforts are successful, as a field we may not only gain a more useful set of peer support technologies, but we also will learn more about how to intervene in a more general sense to achieve meaningful educational outcomes.

HOW CAN PEER SUPPORTS CONTRIBUTE TO OVERALL INCREASES IN A PERSON'S QUALITY OF LIFE?

The primary goal of peer support interventions is to provide a mechanism for meaningful participation in general education classrooms for students with severe disabilities. As was noted in the previous section, we have been effective at meeting these initial goals and there is a clear roadmap for continued progress in expanding a person's social and academic participation in school life. However, even after we have accomplished these goals, how have we changed a person's life? At the end of the day, what matters in life is that a person is happy and makes others happy.

Such a question is really about how we change a person's quality of life. If peer support interventions can allow access into social milieus and align learning objectives with those of other students, how does this affect people's lives at a broader level? Do students with severe disabilities develop more friendships using peer support interventions than they do with more traditional approaches? Do those friendships endure over time? Does learning from the same curriculum as peers without disabilities produce better long-term outcomes and, if so, in what areas? Is it easier for students with severe disabilities to enter the workforce, maintain employment, and continue to learn as a result of having access to the general curriculum? Do the attitudes of peers without disabilities and the perceptions of people with disabilities change to focus on commonalities rather than differences and accommodations rather than exclusion?

The primary goal of peer support interventions is meaningful participation in general education classrooms for students with severe disabilities.

Although these questions are very broad and difficult to measure, they are at the core of what we consider in the United States an effective public education. The Jeffersonian ideal of schools functioning to prepare all people for a participatory democracy is abstract, but it ultimately is what we as educators are attempting to achieve when we discuss inclusion and membership through our educational practices. It would be instructive—and perhaps provide a more compelling case for continued legislative support—if researchers could demonstrate tangible long-term benefits of inclusive education, including the use of peer support interventions. Without this type of "big picture" data, it will be difficult to convince policy makers that these types of intensive, inclusive approaches to educating students with disabilities are worthwhile investments.

HOW CAN RESEARCH CONTRIBUTE TO PEER SUPPORT EFFECTIVENESS AND VICE VERSA?

In the previous two sections of this epilogue, we have briefly discussed how research can contribute to the effectiveness of peer support interventions. In the final section of this epilogue, we would like to note how peer support interventions have contributed to the development of research methodologies and could influence research effectiveness for developing new evidence-based practices.

An interesting aspect of the research on peer support interventions is that it has not been conducted exclusively within one type of experimental methodology. Instead, a range of experimental and interpretative strategies, tactics, and measures have been used to develop an evidence base relating to the effectiveness of peer support interventions. For example, researchers have already employed an array of single subject, experimental group, qualitative, and case study designs to understand how to promote meaningful curricular access and social relationships using peer-mediated strategies. This suggests that multiple methodologies can be used to develop evidence-based practices and that limiting intervention testing to a single methodology is neither necessary, nor particularly advantageous.

In this sense, research on peer support strategies has contributed to viewing how special education evidence-based practices can employ a plurality of approaches to testing intervention effectiveness and efficiency. Such an approach may be instructive for researchers studying other interventions in that the researchers may not want to limit their testing to an overly restrictive methodological set. Instead, they want to employ a range of experimental and interpretative approaches that match the questions being addressed, rather than vice versa. This might prove to be a particularly effective approach to developing evidence-based practices that the larger field of education, as well as other professional disciplines, might adopt.

CONCLUSION

There has been an exciting level of research activity in relation to peer support interventions since the mid-1990s. The research findings strongly support these interventions as effective educational strategies that intersect well with an inclusive approach to educating students with and without disabilities. There are many interesting avenues to pursue in the continued development of these interventions, including expanding the breadth of results, more thoroughly assessing aspects of its social validity, and studying the long-term effects on individuals with and without disabilities. All of this is very exciting.

What makes working in the area of peer supports all the more exciting is the degree to which these strategies are being used by educators. More and more sessions are being conducted at more and more conferences relating to this topic, more and more school districts are requesting technical assistance relating to peer supports, and more and more people are studying how to improve its effectiveness. Peer support interventions have become a vibrant part of the special education literature, and, most exciting of all, this approach can accomplish the goals its proponents espouse. We appreciate your interest in peer support interventions, as well as your taking the time to peruse this book. And, we hope that you will use peer supports in your own work as an educator, family member, or self-advocate.

References

Agran, M., Alper, S., & Wehmeyer, M.L. (2002). Access to the general curriculum for students with significant disabilities: What it means to teachers. *Education and Training in Mental Retardation and Developmental Disabilities, 37*, 123–133.

Agran, M., Cavin, M., Wehmeyer, M., & Palmer, S. (2006). Participation of students with moderate to severe disabilities in general curriculum: The effects of the self-determined learning model of instruction. *Research and Practice for Persons with Severe Disabilities, 31*, 230–241.

Agran, M., Fodor-Davis, J., Moore, S.C., & Martella, R.C. (1992). Effects of peer-delivered self-instructional training on lunch-making work tasks for students with severe disabilities. *Education and Training in Mental Retardation, 27*, 230–240.

Agran, M., Sinclair, T., Alper, S., Cavin, M., Wehmeyer, M., & Hughes, C. (2005). Using self-monitoring to increase following-direction skills of students with moderate to severe disabilities in general education. *Education and Training in Developmental Disabilities, 40*, 3–13.

Ahearn, E. (2006). *Standards-based IEPs: Implementation in selected states.* Alexandria, VA: National Association of State Directors of Special Education.

Alberto, P.A., & Troutman, A.C. (2009). *Applied behavior analysis for teachers* (8th ed.). Upper Saddle River, NJ: Prentice Hall.

Baer, D.M., Wolf, M.M., & Risley, T.R. (1968). Some current dimensions of applied behavior analysis. *Journal of Applied Behavior Analysis, 1*, 91–97.

Baldwin, M.D., & Keating, J.F. (2006). *Teaching in secondary schools: Meeting the challenges of today's adolescents.* Boston: Allyn & Bacon.

Barfield, J., Hannigan-Downs, & Lieberman, L.J. (1998). Implementing a peer tutor program: Strategies for practitioners. *Physical Educator, 55*, 211–221.

Barrett, W., & Randall, L. (2004). Investigating the Circle of Friends approach: Adaptations and implications for practice. *Educational Psychology in Practice, 20*, 353–368.

Bellini, S., Peters, J.K., Brianner, L., & Hopf, A. (2007). A meta-analysis of school-based social skills interventions for children with autism spectrum disorders. *Remedial and Special Education, 28*, 153–162.

Bensted, E.A., & Bachor, D.G. (2002). The academic effects of low achieving or inattentive students providing peer support to students with moderate to severe disabilities in general education classrooms. *Exceptionality Education Canada, 12*, 51–73.

Bijou, S.W., & Baer, D.M. (1961). *Child development.* New York: Appleton-Century-Crofts.

Boardman, A.G., Argüelles, M.E., Vaughn, S., Hughes, M.T., & Klingner, J. (2005). Special education teachers' views of research-based practices. *Journal of Special Education, 39*, 168–180.

Bond, R.J., & Castagnera, E. (2003). Supporting one another: Peer tutoring in an inclusive San Diego high school. In D. Fisher & N. Frey (Eds.), *Inclusive urban schools* (pp. 119–142). Baltimore: Paul H. Brookes Publishing Co.

Bond, R.J., & Castagnera, E. (2006). Peer supports and inclusive education: An underutilized resource. *Theory Into Practice, 45*, 224–229.

Brady, M.P., Shores, R.E., Gunter, P., McEvoy, M.A., Fox, J.J., & White, C. (1985). Generalization of a severely handicapped adolescent's social interaction responses via multiple peers in a classroom setting. *Journal of The Association for Persons with Severe Handicaps, 9*, 278–295.

Breen, C.G., & Haring, T.G. (1992). Effects of contextual competence on social initiations. *Journal of Applied Behavior Analysis, 24*, 337–347.

Broer, S.M., Doyle, M.B., & Giangreco, M.F. (2005). Perspectives of students with intellectual disabilities about their experiences with paraprofessional support. *Exceptional Children, 71*, 415–430.

Browder, D.M., & Cooper-Duffy, K. (2003). Evidence-based practices for students with severe disabilities and the requirements for accountability in "No Child Left Behind." *Journal of Special Education, 37*, 157–163.

Browder, D.M., & Spooner, F. (Eds.). (2006). *Teaching language arts, math, and science to students with significant cognitive disabilities.* Baltimore: Paul H. Brookes Publishing Co.

Browder, D.M., Spooner, F., Algozzine, R., Ahlgrim-Delzell, L., Flowers, C., & Karvonen, M. (2003). What we know and need to know about alternative assessments. *Exceptional Children, 70,* 45–61.

Browder, D.M., Spooner, F., Wakeman, S., Trela, K., & Baker, J.N. (2006). Aligning instruction with academic content standards: Finding the link. *Research and Practice for Persons with Severe Disabilities, 31,* 293–308.

Browder, D.M., Trela, K., & Jimenez, B. (2007). Training teachers to follow a task analysis to engage middle school students with moderate and severe developmental disabilities in grade-appropriate literature. *Focus on Autism and Other Developmental Disabilities, 22,* 206–219.

Browder, D.M., Wakeman, S.Y., Flowers, C, Rickelman, R.J., Pugalee, D., & Karvonen, M. (2007). Creating access to the general curriculum with links to grade-level content for students with significant cognitive disabilities: An explication of the concept. *The Journal of Special Education, 41,* 2–16.

Browder, D.M., Wallace, T., Snell, M.E., & Kleinert, H. (2005). *The use of progress monitoring with students with significant cognitive disabilities: A white paper prepared for the National Center on Student Progress Monitoring.* Washington, DC: National Center on Student Progress Monitoring.

Browder, D.M., & Xin, Y.P. (1998). A meta-analysis and review of sight word research and its implications for teaching functional reading to individuals with moderate and severe disabilities. *Journal of Special Education, 32,* 130–153.

Brown, B.B., & Klute, C. (2003). Friendships, cliques, and crowds. In G.R. Adams & M.D. Berzonsky (Eds.), *Blackwell handbook of adolescence* (pp. 330–348). Malden, MA: Blackwell.

Brown, I., Percy, M., & Machalek, K. (2007). Education for individuals with intellectual and developmental disabilities. In I. Brown & M. Percy (Eds.), *A comprehensive guide to intellectual and developmental disabilities* (pp. 489–510). Baltimore: Paul H. Brookes Publishing Co.

Brown, L., Branston, M., Hamre-Nietupski, S., Johnson, F., Wilcox, B., & Gruenewald, L. (1979). A rationale for comprehensive longitudinal interactions between severely handicapped students and nonhandicapped students and other citizens. *AAESPH Review, 4*(1), 3–14.

Brown, L., Branston, M.B., Hamre-Nietupski, S., Pumpian, I., Certo, N., & Gruenewald, L. (1979). A strategy for developing chronological-age-appropriate and functional curricular content for severely handicapped adolescents and young adults. *Journal of Special Education, 13,* 81–90.

Brown, L., Falvey, M., Vincent, L., Kaye, N., Johnson, F., Ferrara-Parrish, P., et al. (1980). Strategies for generating comprehensive, longitudinal, and chronological-age-appropriate individualized programs for adolescent and young-adult severely handicapped students. *Journal of Special Education, 14,* 199–215.

Brown, L., Farrington, K., Knight, T., Ross, C., & Ziegler, M. (1999). Fewer paraprofessionals and more teachers and therapists in educational programs for students with significant disabilities. *Journal of The Association for Persons with Severe Handicaps, 24,* 250–253.

Butler, F.M., Miller, S.P., Lee, K., & Pierce, T. (2001). Teaching mathematics to students with mild-to-moderate mental retardation: A review of the literature. *Mental Retardation, 39,* 20–31.

Calculator, S.N., & Jorgensen, C.M. (1994). *Including students with severe disabilities in schools: Fostering communication, interaction, and participation.* San Diego: Singular.

Cannella, H.I., O'Reilly, M.F., & Lancioni, G.E. (2005). Choice and preference assessment research with people with severe to profound developmental disabilities: A review of the literature. *Research in Developmental Disabilities, 26,* 1–15.

Carter, E.W., Cushing, L.S., Clark, N.M., & Kennedy, C.H. (2005). Effects of peer support interventions on students' access to the general curriculum and social interactions. *Research and Practice for Persons with Severe Disabilities, 30,* 15–25.

Carter, E.W., Cushing, L.S., & Kennedy, C.H. (2008). Promoting rigor, relevance, and relationships through peer support interventions. *TASH Connections, 34*(2), 20–23.

Carter, E.W., & Hughes, C. (2005). Increasing social interaction among adolescents with intellectual disabilities and their general education peers: Effective interventions. *Research and Practice for Persons with Severe Disabilities, 30,* 179–193.

Carter, E.W., & Hughes, C. (2006). Including high school students with severe disabilities in general education classes: Perspectives of general and special educators, paraprofessionals, and administrators. *Research and Practice for Persons with Severe Disabilities, 31,* 174–185.

Carter, E.W., & Hughes, C. (2007). Social interaction interventions: Promoting socially supportive environments and teaching new skills. In S.L. Odom, R.H. Horner, M. Snell, & J. Blacher (Eds.), *Handbook on developmental disabilities* (pp. 310–329). New York: Guilford Press.

Carter, E.W., Hughes, C., Copeland, S.R., & Breen, C. (2001). Differences between high school students who do and do not volunteer to participate in peer interaction programs. *Journal of The Association for Persons with Severe Handicaps, 26,* 229–239.

Carter, E.W., Hughes, C., Guth, C., & Copeland, S.R. (2005). Factors influencing social interaction among high school students with intellectual disabilities and their general education peers. *American Journal on Mental Retardation, 110,* 366–377.

Carter, E.W., & Kennedy, C.H. (2006). Promoting access to the general curriculum using peer support strategies. *Research and Practice for Persons with Severe Disabilities, 31,* 284–292.

Carter, E.W., Lane, K.L., Pierson, M.R., & Stang, K.K. (2008). Promoting self-determination for transition-age youth: Views of high school general and special educators. *Exceptional Children.*

Carter, E.W., O'Rourke, L., Sisco, L.G., & Pelsue, D. (in press). Knowledge, responsibilities, and training needs of paraprofessionals in elementary and secondary schools. *Remedial and Special Education.*

Carter, E.W., & Pesko, M.J. (2008). Social validity of peer interaction intervention strategies in high school classrooms: Effectiveness, feasibility, and actual use. *Exceptionality,* 16, 156–173.

Carter, E.W., Sisco, L.G., Brown, L., Brickham, D., & Al-Khabbaz, Z. (in press). Peer interactions and academic engagement of youth with developmental disabilities in inclusive middle and high school classrooms. *American Journal on Mental Retardation.*

Carter, E.W., Sisco, L.G., Melekoglu, M., & Kurkowski, C. (in press). Peer supports as an alternative to individually assigned paraprofessionals in inclusive high school classrooms. *Research and Practice for Persons with Severe Disabilities.*

Causton-Theoharis, J., Giangreco, M.F., Doyle, M.B., & Vadasy, P.F. (2007). Paraprofessionals: The "sous chefs" of literacy instruction. *TEACHING Exceptional Children* 40(1), 56–62.

Causton-Theoharis, J.N., & Malmgren, K.W. (2005a). Building bridges: Strategies to help paraprofessionals promote peer interaction. *TEACHING Exceptional Children,* 37(6), 18–24.

Causton-Theoharis, J.N., & Malmgren, K.W. (2005b). Increasing peer interactions for students with severe disabilities via paraprofessional training. *Exceptional Children,* 71, 431–444.

Christensen, L., Young, K.R., & Marchant, M. (2007). Behavioral intervention planning: Increasing appropriate behavior of a socially withdrawn student. *Education and Treatment of Children, 30,* 81–103.

Cipani, E., & Spooner, F. (1994). *Curricular and instructional approaches for people with severe disabilities.* Boston: Allyn & Bacon.

Clark, N.M., Cushing, L.S., & Kennedy, C.H. (2004). An intensive onsite technical assistance model to promote inclusive educational practices for students with disabilities in middle school and high school. *Research and Practice for Persons with Severe Disabilities, 29,* 253–262.

Clayton, J., Burdge, M., Denham, A., Kleinert, H.L., & Kearns, J. (2006). A four-step process for accessing the general curriculum for students with significant cognitive disabilities. *TEACHING Exceptional Children, 8(5),* 20–27.

Coie, J.D., Dodge, K.A., & Kupersmidt, J.B. (1990). Peer group behavior and social status. In S.R. Asher & J.D. Coie (Eds.), *Peer rejection in childhood* (pp. 17–59). New York: Cambridge University Press.

Collins, B.C. (2002). Using peers to facilitate learning by students with moderate disabilities. *The Behavior Analyst Today, 3*(3), 329–341.

Collins, B.C., Branson, T.A., & Hall, M. (1995). Teaching generalized reading of cooking product labels to adolescents with mental disabilities through the use of key words taught by peer tutors. *Education and Training in Mental Retardation and Developmental Disabilities, 30,* 65–75.

Collins, B.C., Branson, T.A., Hall, M., & Rankin, S.W. (2001). Teaching secondary students with moderate disabilities in an inclusive academic classroom setting. *Journal of Developmental and Physical Disabilities, 13,* 41–59.

Conroy, M.A., Asmus, J.M., Ladwig, C.N., Sellers, J.A., & Valcante, G. (2004). The effects of proximity on the classroom behaviors of students with autism in general education settings. *Behavioral Disorders, 29,* 119–129.

Cooper, J.O., Heron, T.E., & Heward, W.L. (2007). *Applied behavior analysis* (2nd ed.). Upper Saddle River, NJ: Pearson.

Copeland, S.R., Hughes, C., Agran, M., Wehmeyer, M.L., & Fowler, S.E. (2002). An intervention package to support high school students with mental retardation in general education classrooms. *American Journal on Mental Retardation, 107,* 32–45.

Copeland, S.R., Hughes, C., Carter, E.W., Guth, C., Presley, J., Williams, C.R., et al. (2004). Increasing access to general education: Perspectives of participants in a high school peer support program. *Remedial and Special Education, 26,* 342–352.

Copeland, S.R., McCall, J., Williams, C.R., Guth, C., Carter, E.W., Fowler, S.E., et al. (2002). High school peer buddies: A win-win situation. *TEACHING Exceptional Children, 35*(1), 16–21.

Council for Exceptional Children. (2003). *What every special educator must know: Ethics, standards, and guidelines for special educators* (5th ed.). Reston, VA: Author.

Council for Exceptional Children. (2004). *The CEC paraeducator standards workbook.* Arlington, VA: Author.

Courtade-Little, G., & Browder, D.M. (2005). *Aligning IEPs with academic standards for students with moderate and severe disabilities*. Verona, WI: Attainment.

Cowie, H., & Wallace, P. (2000). *Peer support in action: From bystanding to standing by*. London: Sage.

Cushing, L.S., Clark, N.M., Carter, E.W., & Kennedy, C.H. (2003). Peer supports and access to the general education curriculum. *TASH Connections, 29*(10), 8–11.

Cushing, L.S., Clark, N.M., Carter, E.W., & Kennedy, C.H. (2005). Access to the general education curriculum for students with severe disabilities: What it means and how to accomplish it. *TEACHING Exceptional Children, 38*(2), 6–13.

Cushing, L.S., & Kennedy, C.H. (1997). Academic effects on students without disabilities who serve as peer supports for students with disabilities in general education classrooms. *Journal of Applied Behavior Analysis, 30,*139–152.

Cushing, L.S., Kennedy, C.H., Shukla, S., Davis, J., & Meyer, K.A. (1997). Disentangling the effects of curriculum revision and social grouping within cooperative learning arrangements. *Focus on Autism and Other Developmental Disabilities, 12*, 231–240.

Danielson, L., & Bellamy, T. (1989). State variation in placement of children with handicaps in segregated environments. *Exceptional Children, 55*, 448–455.

Davis, B., Caros, J., & Carnine, D. (2006). Using technology to access the general education curriculum. In D.D. Deshler & J.B. Schumaker (Eds.), *Teaching adolescents with disabilities: Accessing the general education curriculum* (pp. 187–233). Thousand Oaks, CA: Corwin Press.

Deno, S.L. (2003). Developments in curriculum-based measurement. *Journal of Special Education, 37*, 184–192.

Devlin, P. (2005). Effect of continuous improvement training on student interaction and engagement. *Research and Practice for Persons with Severe Disabilities, 30*, 47–59.

Dover, W.F. (2005). Consult and support students with special needs in inclusive classrooms. *Intervention in School and Clinic, 41*, 32–35.

Downing, J.E. (2005a). Inclusive education for high school students with severe intellectual disabilities: Supporting communication. *Augmentative and Alternative Communication, 21*, 132–148.

Downing, J.E. (2005b). *Teaching communication skills to students with severe disabilities* (2nd ed.). Baltimore: Paul H. Brookes Publishing Co.

Downing, J.E. (2005c). *Teaching literacy to students with significant disabilities: Strategies for the K-12 inclusive classroom*. Thousand Oaks, CA: Corwin Press.

Downing, J.E. (2006). On peer support, universal design, and access to the core curriculum for students with severe disabilities: A personnel preparation perspective. *Research and Practice for Persons with Severe Disabilities, 31*, 327–330.

Downing, J.E. (2008). *Including students with severe and multiple disabilities in typical classrooms: Practical strategies for teachers* (3rd ed.). Baltimore: Paul H. Brookes Publishing Co.

Downing, J.E., Ryndak, D.L., & Clark, D. (2000). Paraeducators in inclusive classrooms: Their own perceptions. *Remedial and Special Education, 21*, 171–181.

Doyle, M.B. (2008). *The paraprofessional's guide to the inclusive classroom: Working as a team* (3rd ed.). Baltimore: Paul H. Brookes Publishing Co.

Dugan, E., Kamps, D., Leonard, B., Watkins, N., Rheinberger, A., & Stackhaus, J. (1995). Effects of cooperative learning groups during social studies for students with autism and fourth-grade peers. *Journal of Applied Behavior Analysis, 28*, 175–188.

Dymond, S.K., Renzaglia, A., & Chun, E. (2007). Elements of effective high school service learning programs that include students with and without disabilities. *Remedial and Special Education, 28*, 227–243.

Dymond, S.K., & Russell, D.L. (2004). Impact of grade and disability on the instructional context of inclusive classrooms. *Education and Training in Developmental Disabilities, 39*, 127–140.

Education for All Handicapped Children Act of 1975, PL 94-142, 20 U.S.C. §§ 1400 *et seq.*

Edyburn, D.L. (2000). Assistive technology and students with mild disabilities. *Focus on Exceptional Children, 32*(9), 1–24.

Evans, I.M., & Meyer, L.H. (2001). Having friendships and Rett syndrome: How social relationships create a meaningful context for limited skills. *Disability and Rehabilitation, 23*, 167–176.

Falvey, M.A. (1995). *Inclusive and heterogeneous schooling: Assessment, curriculum, and instruction*. Baltimore: Paul H. Brookes Publishing Co.

Farlow, L.J., & Snell, M.E. (1989). Teacher use of student performance data to make instructional decisions: Practices in programs for students with moderate to profound disabilities. *Journal of The Association for Persons with Severe Handicaps, 14*, 13–22.

Ferguson, D.L., & Ralph, G.R. (1996). The changing role of special educators: A development waiting for a trend. *Contemporary Education, 68*, 49–51.

Ferster, C.B., & DeMyer, M.K. (1961). The development of performances in autistic children in an automatically controlled environment. *Journal of Chronic Diseases, 13*, 312–345.

Fisher, D. (1999). According to their peers: Inclusion as high school students see it. *Mental Retardation, 37*, 458–467.

Flower, A., Burns, M.K., & Bottsford-Miller, N.A. (2007). Meta-analysis of disability simulation research. *Remedial and Special Education, 28*, 72–79.

Flowers, C., Ahlgrim-Delzell, L., Browder, D., & Spooner, F. (2005). Teachers' perceptions of alternate assessment. *Research and Practice for Persons with Severe Disabilities, 30*, 81–92.

Flowers, C.P., Browder, D.M., Ahlgrim-Delzell, L., & Spooner, F. (2006). Promoting the alignment of curriculum, assessment, and instruction. In D.M. Browder & F. Spooner (Eds.), *Teaching language arts, math, and science to students with significant cognitive disabilities* (pp. 295–311). Baltimore: Paul H. Brookes Publishing Co.

Ford, A., Schnorr, R., Meyer, L., Davern, L., Black, J., & Dempsey, P. (1989). *The Syracuse community-referenced curriculum guide for students with moderate and severe disabilities*. Baltimore: Paul H. Brookes Publishing Co.

Foreman, P., Arthur-Kelly, M., Pascoe, S., & Smith, B.S. (2004). Evaluation the educational experiences of students with profound and multiple disabilities in inclusive and segregated classroom settings: An Australian perspective. *Research and Practice for Persons with Severe Disabilities, 29*, 183–193.

Fox, J.J., Gunter, P., Brady, M.P., Bambara, L.M., Spiegel-McGill, P., & Shores, R.E. (1984). Using multiple peer exemplars to develop generalized social responding of an autistic girl. *Monographs in Behavior Disorders, 7*, 17–26.

Frederickson, N., & Turner, J. (2003). Utilizing the classroom peer group to address children's social needs: An evaluation of the Circle of Friends intervention approach. *Journal of Special Education, 36*, 234–245.

French, N.K. (2001). Supervising paraprofessionals: A survey of teacher practices. *Journal of Special Education, 35*, 41–53.

Friend, M., & Cook, L. (2007). *Interactions: Collaboration skills for school professionals* (5th ed.). Boston: Pearson.

Fryxell, D., & Kennedy, C.H. (1995). Placement along the continuum of services and its impact on students' social relationships. *Journal of The Association for Persons with Severe Handicaps, 20*, 259–269.

Fuller, P.R. (1949). Operant conditioning of a vegetative human organism. *American Journal of Psychology, 62*, 587–590.

Gardner, R., Nobel, M.M., Hessler, T., Yawn, C.D., & Heron, T.E. (2007). Tutoring system innovations: Past practice to future prototypes. *Intervention in School and Clinic, 43*, 71–81.

Garrison-Harrell, L., Kamps, D., & Kravitz, T. (1997). The effects of peer networks on social-communicative behaviors for students with autism. *Focus on Autism and Other Developmental Disabilities, 12*, 241–254.

Gaylord-Ross, R., & Haring, T.G. (1987). Social interaction research for adolescents with severe handicaps. *Behavioral Disorders, 12*, 264–275.

Gaylord-Ross, R.J., Haring, T.G., Breen, C., & Pitts-Conway, V. (1984). The training and generalization of social interaction skills with autistic youth. *Journal of Applied Behavior Analysis, 17*, 229–247.

Gerber, S.B., Finn, J.D., Achilles, C.M., & Boyd-Zaharias, J. (2001). Teacher aides and students' academic achievement. *Educational Evaluation and Policy Analysis, 23*, 123–143.

Ghere, G., York-Barr, J., & Sommerness, J. (2002). *Supporting students with disabilities in inclusive schools: A curriculum for job-embedded paraprofessional development*. Minneapolis: University of Minnesota, Institute on Community Integration and Department of Educational Policy and Administration.

Giangreco, M.F., Backus, L., CichoskiKelly, E., Sherman, P., & Mavropoulos, Y. (2003). Paraeducator training materials to facilitate inclusive education: Initial field-test data. *Rural Special Education Quarterly, 22*, 17–27.

Giangreco, M.F., & Broer, S.M. (2005). Questionable utilization of paraprofessionals in inclusive schools: Are we addressing symptoms or causes? *Focus on Autism and Other Developmental Disabilities, 20*, 10–26.

Giangreco, M.F., & Broer, S.M. (2007). School-based screening to determine overreliance on paraprofessionals. *Focus on Autism and Other Developmental Disabilities, 22*, 149–158.

Giangreco, M.F., Broer, S.M., & Edelman, S.W. (2001). Teacher engagement with students with disabilities: Differences based on paraprofessional service delivery models. *Journal of The Association for Persons with Severe Handicaps, 26*, 75–86.

Giangreco, M.F., & Doyle, M.B. (2007). Teacher assistants in inclusive schools. In L. Florian (Ed.), *The SAGE handbook of special education* (pp. 429–439). London: Sage.

Giangreco, M.F., Edelman, S.W., & Broer, S.M. (2003). Schoolwide planning to improve paraeducator supports. *Exceptional Children, 70*, 63–79.

Giangreco, M.F., Edelman, S.W., Broer, S.M., & Doyle, M.B. (2001). Paraprofessional support of students with disabilities: Literature from the past decade. *Exceptional Children, 68*, 45–64.

Giangreco, M.F., Edelman, S., Luiselli, T.E., & MacFarland, S.Z.C. (1997). Helping or hovering? Effects of instructional assistant proximity on students with disabilities. *Exceptional Children, 64*, 7–18.

Giangreco, M.F., Halvorsen, A., Doyle, M.B., & Broer, S.M. (2004). Alternatives to overreliance on paraprofessionals in inclusive schools. *Journal of Special Education Leadership, 17*, 82–90.

Giangreco, M.F., Suter, J.C., & Doyle, M.B. (in press). Recent research on paraprofessionals in inclusion-oriented schools. *Journal of Educational & Psychological Consultation.*

Giangreco, M.F., Yuan, S., McKenzie, B., Cameron, P., & Fialka, J. (2005). "Be careful what you wish for...": Five reasons to be concerned about the assignment of individual paraprofessionals. *TEACHING Exceptional Children, 37*(5), 28–34.

Gifford-Smith, M.E., & Brownell, C.A. (2003). Childhood peer relationships: Social acceptance, friendships, and peer networks. *Journal of School Psychology, 41,* 235–284.

Gilberts, G.H., Agran, M., Hughes, C., & Wehmeyer, M. (2001). The effects of peer delivered self-monitoring strategies on the participation of students with severe disabilities in general education classrooms. *Journal of The Association for Persons with Severe Handicaps, 26,* 25–36.

Gillies, R.M. (2007). *Cooperative learning: Integrating theory and practice.* Thousand Oaks, CA: Sage.

Ginsburg-Block, M.D., Rohrbeck, C.A., & Fantuzzo, J.W. (2006). A meta-analytic review of social, self-concept, and behavioral outcomes of peer-assisted learning. *Journal of Educational Psychology, 98,* 732–749.

Goldstein, H., Kaczmarek, L.A., & English, K.M. (Vol. Eds.). (2002). *Promoting social communication: Children with developmental disabilities from birth to adolescence.* In S.F. Warren & J. Reichle (Series Eds.), *Communication and language intervention series (Vol. 10).* Baltimore: Paul H. Brookes Publishing Co.

Goldstein, H., & Morgan, L. (2002). Social interaction and models of friendship development. In S.F. Warren & J. Reichle (Series Eds.) & H. Goldstein, L.A. Kaczmarek, & K.M. English (Vol. Eds.), *Communication and language intervention series: Vol. 10. Promoting social communication: Children with developmental disabilities from birth to adolescence* (pp. 5–25). Baltimore: Paul H. Brookes Publishing Co.

Goldstein, H., Schneider, N., & Thiemann, K. (2007). Peer-mediated social communication intervention. *Topics in Language Disorders, 27,* 182–199.

Goldstein, L. (2003, May 28). Disabled by paperwork? *Education Week, 22*(38), 1–2.

Greenwood, C.R., & Abbott, M. (2001). The research to practice gap in special education. *Teacher Education and Special Education, 24,* 276–289.

Greenwood, C.R., Arreaga-Mayer, C., Utley, C.A., Gavin, K.M., & Terry, B.J. (2001). Classwide peer tutoring learning management system: Applications with elementary-level English language learners. *Remedial and Special Education, 22,* 34–47.

Gunter, P.L., & Denny, R.K. (2004). Data collection in research and applications involving students with emotional and behavioral disorders. In R.B. Rutherford, M.M. Quinn, & S.R. Mathur (Eds.), *Handbook of research in emotional and behavioral disorders* (pp. 582–595). New York: Guilford.

Gunter, P.L., Venn, M.L., Patrick, J., Miller, K.A., & Kelly, L. (2003). Efficacy of using momentary time samples to determine on-task behavior of students with emotional/behavioral disorders. *Education and Treatment of Children, 26,* 400–412.

Guskey, T.R. (2007). Multiple sources of evidence: An analysis of stakeholders' perceptions of various indicators of student learning. *Educational Measurement: Issues and Practice, 26,* 19–27.

Halle, J.W., Gabler-Halle, D., & Chung, T.B. (1999). Effects of a peer-mediated aerobic conditioning program on fitness levels of youth with mental retardation: Two systematic replications. *Mental Retardation, 37,* 435–448.

Han, K.G., & Chadsey, J.G. (2004). The influence of gender patterns and grade level on friendship expectations of middle school students toward peers with severe disabilities. *Focus on Autism and Other Developmental Disabilities, 19,* 205–214.

Haring, T.G., & Breen, C.G. (1992). A peer-mediated social network intervention to enhance the social integration of persons with moderate and severe disabilities. *Journal of Applied Behavior Analysis, 25,* 319–333.

Harper, G.F., & Maheady, L. (2007). Peer-mediated teaching and students with learning disabilities. *Intervention in School and Clinic, 43*(2), 101–107.

Harris, F.R., Wolf, M.M., & Baer, D.M. (1964). Effects of adult social reinforcement on child behavior. *Journal of Nursery Education, 20,* 8–17.

Hart, B.M., Reynolds, N.J., Baer, D.M., Brawley, E.R., & Harris, F.R. (1968). Effect of contingent and noncontingent social reinforcement on the cooperative play of a preschool child. *Journal of Applied Behavior Analysis, 1,* 73–76.

Hemmingsson, H., Borell, L., & Gustavsson, A. (2003). Participation in school: School assistants creating opportunities and obstacles for pupils with disabilities. *Occupational Therapy Journal of Research, 23*(3), 88–98.

Hendrickson, J.M., Shokoohi-Yekta, M., Hamre-Nietupski, S., & Gable, R.A. (1996). Middle and high school students' perceptions on being friends with peers with severe disabilities. *Exceptional Children, 63,* 19–28.

Heron, T.E., Villareal, D.M., Ma, Y., Christianson, R.J., & Heron, K.M. (2006). Peer tutoring systems: Applications in classrooms and specialized environments. *Reading and Writing Quarterly, 22,* 27–45.

Heward, W.L. (2003). Ten faulty notions about teaching and learning that hinder the effectiveness of special education. *Journal of Special Education, 36,* 186–205.

Hitchcock, C., Meyer, A., Rose, D., & Jackson, R. (2002). Providing new access to the general curriculum: Universal design for learning. *TEACHING Exceptional Children, 35(2)*, 8–17.

Horner, R.H., Carr, E.G., Halle, J., McGee, G., Odom, S., & Wolery, M. (2005). The use of single subject research to identify evidence-based practice in special education. *Exceptional Children, 71*, 165–179.

Hughes, C., & Carter, E.W. (2008). *Peer buddy programs for successful secondary inclusion.* Baltimore: Paul H. Brookes Publishing Co.

Hughes, C., Carter, E.W., Hughes, T., Bradford, E., & Copeland, S.R. (2002). Effects of instructional versus non-instructional roles on the social interactions of high school students. *Education and Training in Mental Retardation and Developmental Disabilities, 37*, 146–162.

Hughes, C., Copeland, S.R., Agran, M., Wehmeyer, M.L., Rodi, M.S., et al. (2002). Using self-monitoring to improve performance in general education high school classes. *Education and Training in Mental Retardation and Developmental Disabilities, 37*, 262–272.

Hughes, C., Copeland, S.R., Guth, C., Rung, L.L., Hwang, B., Kleeb, G., et al. (2001). General education students' perspectives on their involvement in a high school peer buddy program. *Education and Training in Mental Retardation and Developmental Disabilities, 36*, 343–356.

Hughes, C., Guth, C., Hall, S., Presley, J., Dye, M., & Byers, C. (1999). "They are my best friends:" Peer buddies promote inclusion in high school. *TEACHING Exceptional Children, 31(5)*, 32–37.

Hughes, C., Harmer, M.L., Killian, D.J., & Niarhos, F. (1995). The effects of multiple-exemplar self-instructional training on high school students' generalized conversational interactions. *Journal of Applied Behavior Analysis, 28*, 201–218.

Hughes, C., Lorden, S.W., Scott, S.V., Hwang, B., Derer, K.R., Rodi, M.S., et al. (1998). Identification and validation of critical conversational social skills. *Journal of Applied Behavior Analysis, 31*, 431–436.

Hughes, C., Rung, L.L., Wehmeyer, M.L., Agran, J., Copeland, S.R., & Hwang, B. (2000). Self-prompted communication book use to increase social interaction among high school students. *Journal of The Association for Persons with Severe Handicaps, 25*, 153–166.

Hunt, P., Alwell, M., & Goetz, L. (1991). Establishing conversational exchanges with family and friends: Moving from training to meaningful communication. *Journal of Special Education, 25*, 305–319.

Hunt, P., Alwell, M., Farron-Davis, F., & Goetz, L. (1996). Creating socially supportive environments for fully included students who experience multiple disabilities. *Journal of The Association for Persons with Severe Handicaps, 21*, 53–71.

Hunt, P., Doering, K., Hirose-Hatae, A., Maier, J., & Goetz, L. (2001). Across program collaboration to support students with and without disabilities in a general education classroom. *Journal for The Association for Persons with Severe Handicaps, 26*, 240–256.

Hunt, P., & McDonnell, J. (2007). Inclusive education. In S.L. Odom, R.H. Horner, M. Snell, & J. Blacher (Eds.), *Handbook on developmental disabilities* (pp. 269–291). New York: Guilford Press.

Hunt, P., Soto, G., Maier, J., & Doering, K. (2003). Collaborative teaming to support students at risk and students with severe disabilities in general education classrooms. *Exceptional Children, 69*, 315–332.

Hunt, P., Staub, D., Alwell, M., & Goetz, L. (1994). Achievement by all students within the context of cooperative learning groups. *Journal of The Association for Persons with Severe Handicaps, 19*, 290–301.

Individuals with Disabilities Education Improvement Act of 2004, PL 108–446, 20 U.S.C. §§ 1400 *et seq.*

Jameson, J.M., McDonnell, J., Johnson, J.W., Riesen, T., & Polychronis, S. (2007). A comparison of one-to-one embedded instruction in the general education classroom and one-to-one massed practice instruction in the special education classroom. *Education and Treatment of Children, 30*, 23–44.

Janney, R., & Snell, M.E. (2004). *Teachers' guides to inclusive practices: Modifying schoolwork* (2nd ed.). Baltimore: Paul H. Brookes Publishing Co.

Janney, R., & Snell, M.E. (2006). *Teachers' guides to inclusive practices: Social relationships and peer support* (2nd ed.). Baltimore: Paul H. Brookes Publishing Co.

Janney, R.E., Snell, M.E., Beers, M.K., & Raynes, M. (1995). Integrating students with moderate and severe disabilities into general education classes. *Exceptional Children, 62*, 425–439.

Jitendra, A.K., Edwards, L.L., Choutka, C.M., & Treadway, P.S. (2002). A collaborative approach to planning in the content areas for students with learning disabilities: Accessing the general curriculum. *Learning Disabilities Research & Practice, 17*, 252–267.

Johnson, M. (Ed.). (2006). *Disability awareness—do it right!* Louisville, KY: Avocado Press.

Jones, V. (2007). 'I felt like I did something good'—the impact on mainstream pupils of a peer tutoring programme for children with autism. *British Journal of Special Education, 34*, 3–9.

Jorgensen, C.M. (1996). Designing inclusive curricula right from the start: Practical strategies and examples for the high school classroom. In S. Stainback & W. Stainback (Eds.), *Inclusion: A guide for educators* (pp. 221–236). Baltimore: Paul H. Brookes Publishing Co.

Jussim, L., Smith, A., Madon, S., & Palumbo, P. (1998). Teacher expectations. *Advances in Research on Teaching, 7,* 1–48.

Kamps, D.M., Barbetta, P.M., Leonard, B.R., & Delquadri, J. (1994). Classwide peer tutoring: An integration strategy to improve reading skills and promote peer interactions among students with autism and general education peers. *Journal of Applied Behavior Analysis, 27,* 49–61.

Kamps, D.M., Dugan, E., Potucek, J., & Collins, A. (1999). Effects of cross-age peer tutoring networks among students with autism and general education students. *Journal of Behavioral Education, 9,* 97–115.

Kamps, D.M., Kravits, T., Lopez, A.G., Kemmerer, K., Potucek, J., Harrell, L.G., et al. (1998). What do the peers think? Social validity of peer-mediated programs. *Education and Treatment of Children, 21,* 107–134.

Kamps, D.M., Lopez, A.G., & Golden, C. (2002). School-age children: Putting research into practice. In S.F. Warren & J. Reichle (Series Eds.) & H. Goldstein, L.A. Kaczmarek, & K.M. English (Vol. Eds.), *Communication and language intervention series: Vol. 10. Promoting social communication: Children with developmental disabilities from birth to adolescence* (pp. 279–306). Baltimore: Paul H. Brookes Publishing Co.

Katsiyannis, A., Zhang, D., & Archwamety, T. (2002). Placement and exit patterns for students with mental retardation: An analysis of national trends. *Education and Training in Mental Retardation and Developmental Disabilities, 37,* 134–145.

Kearns, J., Burdge, M.D., Clayton, J., Denham, A.P., & Kleinert, H.L. (2006). How students demonstrate academic performance in portfolio assessment. In D.M. Browder & F. Spooner (Eds.), *Teaching language arts, math, and science to students with significant cognitive disabilities* (pp. 277–293). Baltimore: Paul H. Brookes Publishing Co.

Keefe, E.B., Moore, V.M., & Duff, F.R. (Eds.). (2006). *Listening to the experts: Students with disabilities speak out.* Baltimore: Paul H. Brookes Publishing Co.

Kennedy, C.H. (2001). Social interaction interventions for youth with severe disabilities should emphasize interdependence. *Mental Retardation and Developmental Disabilities Research Reviews, 7,* 122–127.

Kennedy, C.H. (2002a). The maintenance of behavior as an indicator of social validity. *Behavior Modification, 26,* 594–606.

Kennedy, C.H. (2002b). Promoting social-communicative interactions in adolescents. In S.F. Warren & J. Reichle (Series Eds.) & H. Goldstein, L.A. Kaczmarek, & K.M. English (Vol. Eds.), *Communication and language intervention series: Vol. 10. Promoting social communication: Children with developmental disabilities from birth to adolescence* (pp. 307–329). Baltimore: Paul H. Brookes Publishing Co.

Kennedy, C.H. (2004). Social relationships. In C.H. Kennedy & E. Horn (Eds.), *Including students with severe disabilities* (pp. 100–123). Boston: Allyn & Bacon.

Kennedy, C.H. (2005). *Single-case designs for educational research.* Boston: Allyn & Bacon.

Kennedy, C.H., Cushing, L.S., Carter, E.W., & Clark, N.M. (2008). [Social and academic gains of middle and high school with severe disabilities and their peer supports.] Unpublished raw data.

Kennedy, C.H., Cushing, L., & Itkonen, T. (1997). General education participation increases the social contacts and friendship networks of students with severe disabilities. *Journal of Behavioral Education, 7,* 167–189.

Kennedy, C.H., & Fisher, D. (2001). *Inclusive middle schools.* Baltimore: Paul H. Brookes Publishing Co.

Kennedy, C.H., & Haring, T.G. (1993). Teaching choice making during social interactions to students with profound multiple disabilities. *Journal of Applied Behavior Analysis, 26,* 63–76.

Kennedy, C.H., & Horn, E.M. (2004). *Including students with severe disabilities.* Boston: Pearson/Allyn & Bacon.

Kennedy, C.H., & Itkonen, T. (1994). Some effects of regular class participation on the social contacts and social networks of high school students with severe disabilities. *Journal of The Association for Persons with Severe Handicaps, 19,* 1–10.

Kennedy, C.H., Shukla, S., & Fryxell, D. (1997). Comparing the effects of educational placement on the social relationships of intermediate school students with severe disabilities. *Exceptional Children, 64,* 31–47.

Kishi, G.S., & Meyer, L.H. (1994). What children report and remember: A six-year follow-up of the effects of social contact between peers with and without severe disabilities. *Journal of The Association for Persons with Severe Handicaps, 19,* 277–289.

Kleinert, H.L., McGregor, V., Durbin, M., Blandford, T., Jones, K., Owens, J., et al. (2004). Service-learning opportunities that include students with moderate and severe disabilities. *TEACHING Exceptional Children, 37,* 28–34.

Kleinert, H.L., Miracle, S.A., & Sheppard-Jones, K. (2007). Including students with moderate and severe disabilities in extracurricular and community recreation activities: Steps to success. *TEACHING Exceptional Children, 39*(6), 33–38.

Kluth, P., & Schwarz, P. (2008). *"Just give him the whale!" 20 ways to use fascinations, areas of expertise, and strengths to support students with autism.* Baltimore: Paul H. Brookes Publishing Co.

Knackendoffel, E.A. (2005). Collaborative teaming in secondary schools. *Focus on Exceptional Children, 37*(5), 1–16.

Krajewski, J., & Flaherty, T. (2000). Attitudes of high school students toward individuals with mental retardation. *Mental Retardation, 38*, 154–162.

Krajewski, J., & Hyde, M.S. (2000). Comparison of teen attitudes toward individuals with mental retardation between 1987 and 1998: Has inclusion made a difference? *Education and Training in Mental Retardation and Developmental Disabilities, 35*, 284–293.

Krajewski, J., Hyde, M.S., & O'Keefe, M.K. (2002). Teen attitudes toward individuals with mental retardation from 1987 to 1998: Impact of respondent gender and school variables. *Education and Training in Mental Retardation and Developmental Disabilities, 37*, 27–39.

Kronberg, R., York-Barr, J., & Doyle, M.B. (1996). *Module 2: Curriculum as everything students learn in school: Creating a classroom community.* In J. York-Barr (Series Ed.), *Creating inclusive school communities: A staff development series for general and special educators.* Baltimore: Paul H. Brookes Publishing Co.

Lane, H. (1976). *The wild boy of Aveyron.* Cambridge, MA: Harvard University Press.

Lane, K.L., & Beebe-Frankenberger, M. (2004). *School-based interventions: The tools you need to succeed.* Boston: Pearson.

Lane, K. L., Fletcher, T., Carter, E. W., Dejud, C., & DeLorenzo, J. (2007). Paraprofessional-led phonological awareness training with youngsters at-risk for reading and behavioral concerns. *Remedial and Special Education, 28*, 266–276.

Lane, K.L., Pierson, M.R., & Givner, C.C. (2004). Secondary teachers' views on social competence: Skills essential for success. *Journal of Special Education, 38*, 174–186.

Lane, K.L., Pierson, M.R., Stang, K., & Carter, E.W. (in press). Teacher expectations of students' classroom behavior: Do expectations vary as a function of school risk? *Remedial and Special Education.*

Laushey, K.M., & Heflin, L.J. (2000). Enhancing social skills of kindergarten children with autism through the training of multiple peers as tutors. *Journal of Autism and Developmental Disorders, 30*, 183–193.

Lee, S.H., Amos, B.A., Gragoudas, S., Lee, Y., Shogren, K.A., Theoharis, R., et al. (2006). Curriculum augmentation and adaptation strategies to promote access to the general curriculum for students with intellectual and developmental disabilities. *Education and Training in Developmental Disabilities, 41*, 199–212.

Lee, S.H., Soukup, J.H., Little, T.D., & Wehmeyer, M.L. (in press). Student and teacher variables contributing to access to the general education curriculum for students with intellectual and developmental disabilities. *Journal of Special Education.*

Logan, K.R., & Malone, D.M. (1998). Comparing instructional contexts of students with and without disabilities in general education classrooms. *Exceptional Children, 64*, 343–358.

Lohrmann-O'Rourke, S., Browder, D.M., & Brown, F. (2000). Guidelines for conducting socially valid preference assessments. *Journal of The Association for Persons with Severe Handicaps, 25*, 42–53.

Longwill, A. (2002). *High school peer tutoring manual.* Retrieved on March 21, 2008, from http://www.kypeertutoring.org

Longwill, A.W., & Kleinert, H.L. (1998). The unexpected benefits of high school peer tutoring. *TEACHING Exceptional Children, 30*(4), 60–65.

Maheady, L., Harper, G.F., & Mallette, B. (2001). Peer-mediated instruction and interventions and students with mild disabilities. *Remedial and Special Education, 22*, 4–14.

Maheady, L., Harper, G.F., & Mallette, B. (2003). Classwide peer tutoring—Go for it. *Current Practice Alerts, 8*, 1–4.

Malmgren, K.W., & Causton-Theoharis, J.N. (2006). Boy in the bubble: Effects of paraprofessional proximity and other pedagogical decisions on the interactions of a student with behavioral disorders. *Journal of Research in Childhood Education, 20*, 301–312.

Manetti, M., Schneider, B.H., & Siperstein, G. (2001). Social acceptance of children with mental retardation: Testing the contact hypothesis with an Italian sample. *International Journal of Behavioral Development, 25*, 279–286.

Marchand-Martella, N.E., & Martella, R.C. (1992). Generalized effects of a peer-delivered first aid program for students with moderate intellectual disabilities. *Journal of Applied Behavior Analysis, 25*, 841–851.

Marchand-Martella, N.E., & Martella, R. (1993). Evaluating the instructional behaviors of peers with mild disabilities who served as first-aid instructors for students with moderate disabilities. *Child and Family Behavior Therapy, 15*, 1–17.

Marks, S.U., Schrader, C., & Levine, M. (1999). Paraeducator experiences in inclusive settings: Helping, hovering, or holding their own? *Exceptional Children, 65*, 315–328.

Martella, R.C., Marchand-Martella, N.E., Miller, T.L., Young, K.R., & Macfarlane, C.A. (1995). Teaching instructional aides and peer tutors to decrease problem behaviors in the classroom. *TEACHING Exceptional Children, 27*(2), 53–56.

Martin, J.E., Van Dycke, J.L., Christensen, W.R., Greene, B.A., Gardner, J.E., & Lovett, D.L. (2006). Increasing student participation in IEP meetings: Establishing self-directed IEP as an evidence-based practice. *Exceptional Children, 72,* 299–316.

Martin, J.E., Van Dycke, J.L., Greene, B.A., Gardner, J.E., Christensen, W.R., Woods, L.L., et al. (2006). Direct observation of teacher-directed IEP meetings: Establishing the need for student IEP meeting instruction. *Exceptional Children, 72,* 187–200.

Martini-Scully, D., Bray, M.A., & Kehle, T.J. (2000). A packaged intervention to reduce disruptive behaviors in general education students. *Psychology in the Schools, 37,* 149–136.

Mastropieri, M.A. (2001). Is the glass half full or half empty? Challenges encountered by first-year special education teachers. *Journal of Special Education, 35,* 66–74.

Mastropieri, M.A., Scruggs, T.E., & Berkeley, S.L. (2007). Peers helping peers. *Educational Leadership, 64*(5), 54–58.

McConnell, S.R. (2002). Interventions to facilitate social interaction for young children with autism: Review of available research and recommendations for educational intervention and future research. *Journal of Autism and Developmental Disorders, 32,* 351–372.

McDonnell, J., Johnson, J.W., Polychronis, S., & Risen, T. (2002). Effects of embedded instruction on students with moderate disabilities enrolled in general education classes. *Education and Training in Mental Retardation and Developmental Disabilities, 37,* 363–377.

McDonnell, J., Mathot-Buckner, C., Thorson, N., & Fister, S. (2001). Supporting the inclusion of students with moderate and severe disabilities in junior high school general education classes: The effects of classwide peer tutoring, multi-element curriculum, and accommodations. *Education and Treatment of Children, 24,* 141–160.

McIntyre, L.L., Kraemer, B.R., Blacher, J., & Simmerman, S. (2004). Quality of life for young adults with severe intellectual disability: Mother's thoughts and reflections. *Journal of Intellectual & Developmental Disability, 29,* 131–146.

McMaster, K.L., Fuchs, D., & Fuchs, L.S. (2006). Research on peer-assisted learning strategies: The promise and limitations of peer-mediated instruction. *Reading & Writing Quarterly, 22,* 5–25.

McSheehan, M., Sonnenmeier, R.M., Jorgensen, C.M., & Turner, K. (2006). Beyond communication access: Promoting learning of the general curriculum by students with significant disabilities. *Topics in Language Disorders, 26,* 266–290.

Meyer, L.M. (2001). The impact of inclusion on children's lives: Multiple outcomes, and friendships, in particu-

lar. *International Journal of Disability, Development, and Education, 48,* 9–31.

Milby, J.B. (1970). Modification of extreme social isolation by contingent social reinforcement. *Journal of Applied Behavior Analysis, 3,* 149–152.

Miller, K.D., Schleien, S.J., & Bedini, L.A. (2003). Barriers to the inclusion of volunteers with developmental disabilities. *Journal of Volunteer Administration, 21,* 25–30.

Miller, M.C., Cooke, N.L., Test, D.W., & White, R. (2003). Effects of friendship circles on the social interactions of elementary age students with mild disabilities. *Journal of Behavioral Education, 12,* 167–184.

Mills, M. (1994). The consultative role of the school based resource teachers. *B.C. Journal of Special Education, 18,* 181–189.

Miracle, S.A., Collins, B.C., Schuster, J.W., & Grisham-Brown, J. (2001). Peer- versus teacher-delivered instruction: Effects on acquisition and maintenance. *Education and Training in Mental Retardation and Developmental Disabilities, 36,* 373–385.

Montessori, M. (1912). *The Montessori method* (A. George, Trans.). New York: Stokes.

Montgomery, L., Benito, N., Valdes, C., Magers, S., & Taluga, K. (2005). *Social inclusion project: A guide to including students with developmental disabilities in middle and high school social activities.* Tallahassee: Florida Developmental Disabilities Council.

Mortweet, S.L., Utley, C.A., Walker, D., Dawson, H.L., Delquadri, J.C., Reddy, S.S., et al. (1999). Classwide peer tutoring: Teaching students with mild mental retardation in inclusive classrooms. *Exceptional Children, 65,* 524–536.

Mu, K., Siegel, E.B., & Allinder, R.M. (2000). Peer interactions and sociometric status of high school students with moderate or severe disabilities in general education classrooms. *Journal of The Association for Persons with Severe Handicaps, 25,* 142–152.

National Council for Accreditation of Teacher Education. (2000). *Professional standards for the accreditation of schools, colleges, and departments of education.* Washington, DC: Author.

No Child Left Behind Act of 2001, PL 107-110, 115 Stat. 1425, 20 U.S.C. §§ 6301 *et seq.*

Odom, S.L., McConnell, S.R., & Chandler, L.K. (1994). Acceptability and feasibility of classroom-based social interaction interventions for young children with disabilities. *Exceptional Children, 60,* 226–236.

Odom, S.L., McConnell, S.R., & McEvoy, M.A. (1992). *Social competence of young children with disabilities: Issues and strategies for intervention.* Baltimore: Paul H. Brookes Publishing Co.

Odom, S.L., & Strain, P.S. (1986). A comparison of peer-initiation and teacher-antecedent interventions for promoting reciprocal social interaction of autistic preschoolers. *Journal of Applied Behavior Analysis, 19*, 59–71.

Ohtake, Y. (2003). Increasing class membership of students with severe disabilities through contribution to classmates' learning. *Research and Practice for Persons with Severe Disabilities, 28*, 228–231.

Orsmond, G.I., Krauss, M.W., & Seltzer, M.M. (2004). Peer relationships and social and recreational activities among adolescents and adults with autism. *Journal of Autism and Developmental Disorders, 34*, 245–256.

Overton, S., & Rausch, J.L. (2002). Peer relationships as support for children with disabilities: An analysis of mothers' goals and indicators for friendship. *Focus on Autism and Other Developmental Disabilities, 17*, 11–29.

Palmer, D.S., Fuller, K., Arora, T., & Nelson, M. (2001). Taking sides: Parent views on inclusion for their children with severe disabilities. *Exceptional Children, 67*, 467–484.

Patterson, K.B. (2006). Roles and responsibilities of paraprofessionals: In their own words. *TEACHING Exceptional Children Plus, 2*(5), 1–13.

Peck, C.A., Donaldson, J., & Pezzoli, M. (1990). Some benefits nonhandicapped adolescents perceive for themselves from their social relationships with peers who have severe handicaps. *Journal of The Association for Persons with Severe Handicaps, 15*, 241–249.

Peck, C.A., Staub, D., Gallucci, C., & Schwartz, I. (2004). Parent perception of the impacts of inclusion on their nondisabled child. *Research and Practice for Persons with Severe Disabilities, 29*, 135–143.

Prater, M.A., Bruhl, S., & Serna, L.A. (1998). Acquiring social skills through cooperative learning and teacher-directed instruction. *Remedial and Special Education, 19*, 160–172.

President's Commission on Excellence in Special Education. (2002). *A new era: Revitalizing special education for children and their families.* Washington, DC: U.S. Department of Education, Office of Special Education and Rehabilitative Services.

Ragland, E.U., Kerr, M.M., & Strain, P.S. (1978). Behavior of withdrawn autistic children. *Behavior Modification, 2*, 565–578.

Rice, N., Drame, E., Owen, L., & Frattura, E.M. (2007). Co-instructing at the secondary level. *TEACHING Exceptional Children, 39*(6), 12–18.

Rillotta, F., & Nettelbeck, T. (2007). Effects of an awareness program on attitudes of students without an intellectual disability towards persons with an intellectual disability. *Journal of Intellectual & Developmental Disability, 32*, 19–27.

Roach, V., Salisbury, C., & McGregor, G. (2002). Applications of a policy framework to evaluate and promote large-scale change. *Exceptional Children, 68*, 451–464.

Robinson, D.R., Schofield, J.W., & Steers-Wentzell, K.L. (2005). Peer and cross-age tutoring in math: Outcomes and their design implications. *Educational Psychology Review, 17*, 327–362.

Ryndak, D.L., & Alper, S. (2002). *Curriculum and instruction for students with significant disabilities in inclusive settings* (2nd ed.). Boston: Allyn & Bacon.

Ryndak, D.L., & Billingsley, F. (2004). Access to the general education curriculum. In C.H. Kennedy & E.M. Horn (Eds.), *Including students with severe disabilities* (pp. 33–53). Boston: Pearson.

Ryndak, D., & Fisher, D. (Eds.). (2003). *The foundations of inclusive education: A compendium of articles on effective strategies to achieve inclusive education* (2nd ed.). Baltimore: TASH.

Salisbury, C.L., Gallucci, C.L., Palombaro, M.M., & Peck, C.A. (1995). Strategies that promote social relations among elementary students with and without severe disabilities in inclusive schools. *Exceptional Children, 62*, 125–137.

Sandall, S.R., Schwartz, I.S., & Lacroix, B. (2004). Interventionists' perspectives about data collection in integrated early childhood classrooms. *Journal of Early Intervention, 26*, 161–174.

Sandstrom, M.J., & Zakriski, A.L. (2004). Understanding the experience of peer rejection. In J.B. Kupersmidt & K.A. Dodge (Eds.), *Children's peer relations: From development to intervention* (pp. 101–118). Washington, DC: American Psychological Association.

Sapon-Shevin, M. (1999). *Because we can change the world: A practical guide to building cooperative, inclusive classroom communities.* Boston: Allyn & Bacon.

Sapon-Shevin, M. (2000/2001). Schools fit for all. *Educational Leadership, 58*(4), 34–39.

Sasso, G.M., Mundschenk, N.A., Melloy, K.J., & Casey, S.D. (1998). A comparison of the effects of organismic and setting variables on the social interaction behavior of children with developmental disabilities and autism. *Focus on Autism and Other Developmental Disabilities, 13*, 2–16.

Sasso, G.M., & Rude, H.A. (1987). Unprogrammed effects of training high-status peers to interact with severely handicapped children. *Journal of Applied Behavior Analysis, 20*, 35–44.

Schloss, P.J., & Kobza, S.A. (1997). The use of peer tutoring for the acquisition of functional math skills among students with moderate retardation. *Education and Treatment of Children, 20*, 189–208.

Schnorr, R.F. (1997). From enrollment to membership: "Belonging" in middle and high school classes. *Journal of The Association for Persons with Severe Handicaps, 22*, 1–15.

Schwartz, I.S., & Baer, D.M. (1991). Social validity assessments: Is current practice state of the art? *Journal of Applied Behavior Analysis, 24,* 189–204.

Séguin, E. (1856). Origin of the treatment and training of idiots. *American Journal of Education, 2,* 145–152.

Shukla, S., Kennedy, C.H., & Cushing, L.S. (1998). Component analysis of peer support strategies: Adult influence on the participation of peers without disabilities. *Journal of Behavioral Education, 8,* 397–413.

Shukla, S., Kennedy, C.H., & Cushing, L.S. (1999). Intermediate school students with severe disabilities: Supporting their social participation in general education classrooms. *Journal of Positive Behavior Interventions, 1,* 130–140.

Siperstein, G.N., Leffert, J.S., & Wenz-Gross, M. (1997). The quality of friendships between children with and without mental retardation. *American Journal on Mental Retardation, 102,* 55–70.

Siperstein, G.N., Norins, J., & Mohler, A. (2007). Social acceptance and attitude change: Fifty years of research. In J.W. Jacobson, J.A. Mulick, & J. Rojahn (Eds.), *Handbook of intellectual and developmental disabilities* (pp. 133–154). New York: Springer.

Siperstein, G.N., Parker, R.C., Bardon, J.N., & Widaman, K.F. (2007). A national study of youth attitudes toward the inclusion of students with intellectual disabilities. *Exceptional Children, 73,* 435–455.

Skär, L., & Tamm, M. (2001). My assistant and I: Disabled children's and adolescents' roles and relationships to their assistants. *Disability & Society, 16,* 917–931.

Skrtic, T.M. (1991). The special education paradox: Equity as the way to excellence. *Harvard Educational Review, 61,* 148–206.

Smith, A. (2006). Access, participation, and progress in the general curriculum in the least restrictive environment for students with significant cognitive disabilities. *Research and Practice for Persons with Severe Disabilities, 31,* 331–336.

Snell, M.E. (2003). Applying research to practice: The more pervasive problem? *Research and Practice for Persons with Severe Disabilities, 28,* 143–147.

Snell, M.E., & Brown, F. (Eds.). (2006). *Instruction of students with severe disabilities* (6th ed.). Upper Saddle River, NJ: Pearson/Merrill/Prentice Hall.

Spencer, V.G. (2006). Peer tutoring and students with emotional or behavioral disorders: A review of the literature. *Behavioral Disorders, 31,* 204–222.

Spooner, F., Dymond, S.K., Smith, A., & Kennedy, C.H. (2006). What we know and need to know about accessing the general curriculum for students with significant cognitive disabilities. *Research and Practice for Persons with Severe Disabilities, 31,* 277–283.

Stainback, S., & Stainback, W. (1992). *Curriculum considerations in inclusive classrooms: Facilitating learning for all students.* Baltimore: Paul H. Brookes Publishing Co.

Stainback, S.B., Stainback, W.C., & Harris, K.C. (1989). Support facilitation: An emerging role for special educators. *Teacher Education and Special Education, 12,* 148–153.

Staub, D., & Hunt, P. (1993). The effects of social interaction training on high school peer tutors of schoolmates with severe disabilities. *Exceptional Children, 60,* 41–57.

Staub, D., Spaulding, M., Peck, C.A., Gallucci, C., & Schwartz, I. (1996). Using nondisabled peers to support the inclusion of students with disabilities at the junior high school level. *Journal of The Association for Persons with Severe Handicaps, 21,* 194–205.

Stenhoff, D.M., & Lignugaris, B. (2007). A review of the effects of peer tutoring on students with mild disabilities in secondary settings. *Exceptional Children, 74,* 8–30.

Strain, P.S., & Timm, M.A. (1974). An experimental analysis of social interaction between a behaviorally disordered preschool child and her classroom peers. *Journal of Applied Behavior Analysis, 7,* 583–590.

Study of Personnel Needs in Special Education. (2002). *The role of paraprofessionals in special education.* Rockville, MD: Westat.

Sussman, S., Pokhrel, P., Ashmore, R.D., & Brown, B.B. (2007). Adolescent peer group identification and characteristics: A review of the literature. *Addictive Behaviors, 32,* 1602–1627.

Suter, J.C., & Giangreco, M.F. (in press). Numbers that count: Exploring special education and paraprofessional service delivery in inclusion-oriented schools. *Journal of Special Education.*

Sutherland, K.S., Alder, N., & Gunter, P.L. (2003). The effects of varying rates of opportunities to respond on the classroom behavior of students with EBD. *Journal of Emotional and Behavioral Disorders, 11,* 239–247.

Sutherland, K.S., Copeland, S., & Wehby, J.H. (2001). Catch them while you can: Monitoring and increasing your rate of praise. *Beyond Behavior, 11,* 46–49.

Swaim, K.F., & Morgan, S.B. (2001). Children's attitudes and behavioral intentions toward a peer with autistic behaviors: Does a brief educational intervention have an effect? *Journal of Autism and Developmental Disorders, 31,* 195–205.

Test, D.W., Mason, C., Hughes, C., Konrad, M., Neale, M., & Wood, W.M. (2004). Student involvement in individualized education program meetings. *Exceptional Children, 70,* 391–412.

Trent, J.W. (1994). *Inventing the feeble mind: A history of mental retardation in the United States.* Berkeley: University of California Press.

Turnbull, H.R., Turnbull, A.P., Wehmeyer, M.L., & Park, J.

(2003). A quality of life framework for special education outcomes. *Remedial and Special Education, 24,* 67–74.

Umbreit, J., Lane, K.L., & Dejud, C. (2004). Improving classroom behavior by modifying task difficulty: Effects of increasing the difficulty of too-easy tasks. *Journal of Positive Behavioral Interventions, 6,* 13–20.

U.S. Department of Education. (2005). *Twenty-seventh annual report to Congress on the implementation of the Individuals with Disabilities Education Act.* Washington, DC: Author.

U.S. Department of Education. (2007). *Description and employment criteria of instructional paraprofessionals: Issue brief.* Washington, DC: National Center for Education Statistics.

Van der Klift, E., & Kunc, N. (2002). Beyond benevolence: Supporting genuine friendship in inclusive schools. In J.S. Thousand, R.A. Villa, & A.I. Nevin (Eds.), *Creativity and collaborative learning: The practical guide to empowering students, teachers, and families* (2nd ed., pp. 21–28). Baltimore: Paul H. Brookes Publishing Co.

Vandercook, T. (1991). Leisure instruction outcomes: Criterion performance, positive interactions, and acceptance by typical high school peers. *The Journal of Special Education, 25,* 320–339.

Villalobos, P.J., Tweit-Hull, D., & Wong, A. (2002). Creating and supporting peer tutoring partnerships in secondary schools. In J.S. Thousand, R.A. Villa, & A.I. Nevin (Eds.), *Creativity and collaborative learning: The practical guide to empowering students, teachers, and families* (pp. 379–403). Baltimore: Paul H. Brookes Publishing Co.

Wagner, M., Cadwallader, T., & Marder, C. (2003). *Life outside the classroom for youth with disabilities: A report from the National Longitudinal Transition Study-2.* Menlo Park, CA: SRI International.

Wagner, M., Newman, L., Cameto, R., Levine, P., & Marder, C. (2003). *Going to school: instructional contexts, programs, and participation of secondary school students with disabilities. A report from the National Longitudinal Transition Study-2 (NLTS2).* Menlo Park, CA: SRI International.

Wallace, T. (2003). *Paraprofessionals.* Gainesville: University of Florida, Center on Personnel Studies in Special Education.

Ward, P., & Ayvazo, S. (2006). Classwide peer tutoring in physical education: Assessing its effects with kindergartners with autism. *Adapted Physical Education Quarterly, 23,* 233–244.

Wehmeyer, M.L. (2006). Beyond access: Ensuring progress in the general education curriculum for students with severe disabilities. *Research and Practice for Persons with Severe Disabilities, 31,* 322–326.

Wehmeyer, M.L., & Agran, M. (2006). Promoting access to the general curriculum for students with significant cognitive disabilities. In D.M. Browder & F. Spooner (Eds.), *Teaching language arts, math, and science to students with significant cognitive disabilities* (pp. 15–37). Baltimore: Paul H. Brookes Publishing Co.

Wehmeyer, M.L., Agran, M., Hughes, C., Martin, J., Mithaug, D.E., & Palmer, S. (2007). *Promoting self-determination in students with intellectual and developmental disabilities.* New York: Guilford Press.

Wehmeyer, M.L., & Field, S. (2007). *Self-determination: Instructional and assessment strategies.* Thousand Oaks, CA: Corwin Press.

Wehmeyer, M.L., Hughes, C., Agran, M., Garner, N., & Yeager, D. (2003). Student-directed learning strategies to promote the progress of students with intellectual disability in inclusive classrooms. *International Journal of Inclusive Education, 7,* 415–428.

Wehmeyer, M.L., Lattin, D.L., Lapp-Rincker, G., & Agran, M. (2003). Access to the general curriculum of middle school students with mental retardation: An observational study. *Remedial and Special Education, 24,* 262–272.

Wehmeyer, M.L., & Patton, J.R. (1999). *Mental retardation in the 21st century.* Austin, TX: PRO-ED.

Wehmeyer, M.L., & Sands, D.J. (Eds.). (1998). *Making it happen: Student involvement in education planning, decision making, and instruction.* Baltimore: Paul H. Brookes Publishing Co.

Wehmeyer, M.L., Sands, D.J., Knowlton, E., & Kozleski, E.B. (2002). *Teaching students with mental retardation: Providing access to the general curriculum.* Baltimore: Paul H. Brookes Publishing Co.

Weiner, J.S. (2005). Peer-mediated conversational repair in students with moderate and severe disabilities. *Research and Practice for Persons with Severe Disabilities, 30,* 26–37.

Westling, D.L., & Fox, L. (2004). *Teaching students with severe disabilities.* Upper Saddle River, NJ: Prentice Hall.

Whitaker, P., Barratt, P., Joy, H., Potter, M., & Thomas, G. (1998). Children with autism and peer group support: Using "circles of friends." *British Journal of Special Education, 25,* 60–64.

Will, M. (1986). Educating children with learning problems: A shared responsibility. *Exceptional Children, 52,* 411–416.

Williams, L.J., & Downing, J.E. (1998). Membership and belonging in inclusive classrooms: What do middle school students have to say? *Journal of The Association for Persons with Severe Handicaps, 23,* 98–110.

Williamson, P., McLeskey, J., Hoppey, D., & Rentz, T.

(2006). Educating students with mental retardation in general education classrooms. *Exceptional Children, 72,* 347–361.

Wolery, M., Anthony, L., Snyder, E.S., Werts, M.G., & Katzenmeyer, J. (1997). Training elementary teachers to embed instruction during classroom activities. *Education and Treatment of Children, 20,* 40–58.

Wolery, M., Bailey, D.B., & Sugai, G.M. (1988). *Effective teaching: Principles and procedures of applied behavior analysis with exceptional students.* Boston: Allyn & Bacon.

Wolf, M.M. (1978). Social validity: The case for subjective measurement or How applied behavior analysis is finding its heart. *Journal of Applied Behavior Analysis, 11,* 203–214.

Wolf, M.M., Risley, T.R., & Mees, H. (1964). Application of operant conditioning procedures to the behavior problems of an autistic child. *Behaviour Research and Therapy, 1,* 305–312.

Wolfensberger, W. (2008). The fiftieth anniversary of what appears to be the world's first doctoral degree program in mental retardation: Some reminiscences of an early graduate. *Intellectual and Developmental Disabilities, 46,* 64–79.

York, J., & Tundidor, H. (1995). Issues raised in the name of inclusion: Perspectives of educators, parents, and students. *Journal of The Association for Persons with Severe Handicaps, 20,* 31–44.

Appendix

Photocopiable Forms

Classroom Activities Assessment

IEP Matrix

Embedded Goals Chart

Screening Questions for Prospective Peers

Peer Support Planning Grid

Checklist for Monitoring Peer Support Arrangements

Opportunities for Communication

Reflection Questions for Students with Disabilities

Reflection Questions for Peers

Reflection Questions for Paraprofessionals and Educators

Classroom Activities Assessment

Class: _____   Student: _____

Teacher: _____   Team: _____

Typical activities and routines	Expectations for students	Adaptations and supports
Whole-class instruction		
Small-group instruction		
Independent work		

(continued)

From Janney, R., & Snell, M.E. (2004). *Modifying schoolwork* (p. 64). Baltimore: Paul H. Brookes Publishing Co.; adapted by permission.

In *Peer Support Strategies for Improving All Students' Social Lives and Learning*
by Erik W. Carter, Lisa S. Cushing, & Craig H. Kennedy
(2009, Paul H. Brookes Publishing Co.)

Typical activities and routines	Expectations for students	Adaptations and supports
Independent work		
Homework		
Assessment		
Needed materials		
Other expectations		

From Janney, R., & Snell, M.E. (2004). *Modifying schoolwork* (p. 64). Baltimore: Paul H. Brookes Publishing Co.; adapted by permission.

Peer Support Strategies for Improving All Students' Social Lives and Learning
by Erik W. Carter, Lisa S. Cushing, & Craig H. Kennedy
(2009, Paul H. Brookes Publishing Co.)

◆ IEP Matrix

Student: _____   Semester/school year: _____

Individualized goals	Daily schedule								

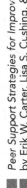

Source: Kennedy and Fisher (2001).

Peer Support Strategies for Improving All Students' Social Lives and Learning
by Erik W. Carter, Lisa S. Cushing, & Craig H. Kennedy
Copyright © 2009 by Paul H. Brookes Publishing Co. All rights reserved.

Embedded Goals Chart

Class: _____   Student: _____

Teacher: _____   Team: _____

Priority goals	When can this goal be addressed?	How will progress be evaluated?

Peer Support Strategies for Improving All Students' Social Lives and Learning
by Erik W. Carter, Lisa S. Cushing, & Craig H. Kennedy
Copyright © 2009 by Paul H. Brookes Publishing Co. All rights reserved.

Screening Questions for Prospective Peers

Person filling out this form: _____ Semester: _____

How well do you already know _____ [student with whom the peer will work]?

What interests you most about becoming a peer support?

What expectations do you have?

What have been your past experiences with your schoolmates with disabilities?

What qualities do you think make for an effective peer support?

Are there aspects of the experience you are concerned about?

(continued)

Peer Support Strategies for Improving All Students' Social Lives and Learning
by Erik W. Carter, Lisa S. Cushing, & Craig H. Kennedy
Copyright © 2009 by Paul H. Brookes Publishing Co. All rights reserved.

What do you think it takes to be an effective peer support?

What school and community activities are you involved in?

What other time commitments do you have this semester?

What experiences have you had that you feel would make you a good peer support?

What questions do you have about becoming a peer support?

Have you had similar experiences in the past?

What do you expect to gain as a result of becoming a peer support?

Have you ever received support from your classmates? Describe the experience.

Peer Support Strategies for Improving All Students' Social Lives and Learning
by Erik W. Carter, Lisa S. Cushing, & Craig H. Kennedy
Copyright © 2009 by Paul H. Brookes Publishing Co. All rights reserved.

Peer Support
Planning Grid

Student: _____   Semester: _____

Daily schedule	Week				
	Monday	Tuesday	Wednesday	Thursday	Friday
Club:					
Club:					
Other:					
Other:					

Peer Support Strategies for Improving All Students' Social Lives and Learning
by Erik W. Carter, Lisa S. Cushing, & Craig H. Kennedy
Copyright © 2009 by Paul H. Brookes Publishing Co. All rights reserved.

Checklist for Monitoring Peer Support Arrangements

Class: _____   Student: _____

Teacher: _____   Team: _____

At various times during the class, reflect on each question and check the associated box when the answer is *yes*. If no boxes are checked for a question, use the space at the bottom of the chart to brainstorm ideas for addressing this item.

Segment of class

1	2	3	4	Reflection questions
❑	❑	❑	❑	Is the student seated next to the peer(s) with whom he or she is paired?
❑	❑	❑	❑	Does the student have the same materials as his or her classmates (e.g., worksheets, books, lab materials, writing utensils, computers)?
❑	❑	❑	❑	Are the student and his or her peers *actively engaged* in ongoing instruction?
❑	❑	❑	❑	Is the work the student is doing *closely aligned* with work expected of the rest of the class?
❑	❑	❑	❑	Are interactions among the student and his or her peers *appropriate* given the context or the types of interactions other students have?
❑	❑	❑	❑	Are students completing class activities in a timely fashion or at a reasonable pace?
❑	❑	❑	❑	Are peers restating or clarifying directions?
❑	❑	❑	❑	Are peers giving appropriate prompts and feedback to the student?
❑	❑	❑	❑	Are peers summarizing activities?
❑	❑	❑	❑	Do the student and his or her peers appear to be enjoying working together?
❑	❑	❑	❑	Are students truly working *together* (rather than simply next to each other)?
❑	❑	❑	❑	Other: _____
❑	❑	❑	❑	Other: _____

Ideas:

Peer Support Strategies for Improving All Students' Social Lives and Learning
by Erik W. Carter, Lisa S. Cushing, & Craig H. Kennedy
Copyright © 2009 by Paul H. Brookes Publishing Co. All rights reserved.

Opportunities for Communication

Student: _____ Semester: _____

Person filling out this form: _____

Does the student have a means to initiate an interaction? How?

Does the student have opportunities to initiate an interaction? When? With whom?

Do others in the environment understand and respond to the student?

Does the student have a means to engage in different functions of communication, or does he or she primarily make requests or protests?

(continued)

From Downing, J.E. (2005). *Teaching communication skills to students with severe disabilities* (2nd ed., p. 33). Baltimore: Paul H. Brookes Publishing Co.; reprinted by permission.

In *Peer Support Strategies for Improving All Students' Social Lives and Learning* by Erik W. Carter, Lisa S. Cushing, & Craig H. Kennedy (2009, Paul H. Brookes Publishing Co.)

Does the student have things to talk about? What are they?

Does the student have the means to respond to others and maintain conversation? How?

Does the student have a way to correct a communication breakdown? How?

From Downing, J.E. (2005). *Teaching communication skills to students with severe disabilities* (2nd ed., p. 33). Baltimore: Paul H. Brookes Publishing Co.; reprinted by permission.

 In *Peer Support Strategies for Improving All Students' Social Lives and Learning* by Erik W. Carter, Lisa S. Cushing, & Craig H. Kennedy (2009, Paul H. Brookes Publishing Co.)

Reflection Questions
for Students with Disabilities

Student: _____ Semester: _____

Are you enjoying spending time with _____? Why or why not?

What are some of the things you do together?

What do you find most helpful? Least helpful?

What do you like or dislike about the supports you receive?

What have you learned from working with _____?

How has _____ benefited from getting to know you?

(continued)

Sources: Broer, Doyle, and Giangreco (2005); Hughes and Carter (2008); Hughes et al. (1999); Hughes et al. (2000).

Peer Support Strategies for Improving All Students' Social Lives and Learning
by Erik W. Carter, Lisa S. Cushing, & Craig H. Kennedy
Copyright © 2009 by Paul H. Brookes Publishing Co. All rights reserved.

❖ Reflection Questions for Students with Disabilities *(continued)*

Do you consider _____ to be a friend?

Is there any other help you think you would need in this class?

Would you like to continue working with _____ ? If not, why not?

Do you do things with _____ outside of school?

Are there other things you would like to do with _____ outside of the class?

Have you made other new friends in this class? Elsewhere in school?

What would you like your teachers to know about how best to support you in class?

Sources: Broer, Doyle, and Giangreco (2005); Hughes and Carter (2008); Hughes et al. (1999); Hughes et al. (2000).

Peer Support Strategies for Improving All Students' Social Lives and Learning
by Erik W. Carter, Lisa S. Cushing, & Craig H. Kennedy
Copyright © 2009 by Paul H. Brookes Publishing Co. All rights reserved.

Reflection Questions
for Peers

Person filling out this form: _____

Partner's name: _____ Semester: _____

How would you describe your experience working with your partner?

Did you enjoy serving in this role? In what ways? What did you like most?

What things have been going really well? Not so well?

Were there aspects of this role you particularly enjoyed? Found difficult?

In what ways have you benefited from participating in this way? What have you learned?

How effective do you feel you are in this role? Are you comfortable with your responsibilities?

What changes have you noticed in your partner, if any?

(continued)

Sources: Bond and Castagnera (2003); Copeland et al. (2004); Hughes et al. (2001); Jones (2007); Kamps et al. (1998); Williams and Downing (1998).

Peer Support Strategies for Improving All Students' Social Lives and Learning by Erik W. Carter, Lisa S. Cushing, & Craig H. Kennedy Copyright © 2009 by Paul H. Brookes Publishing Co. All rights reserved.

Do you think this was a beneficial experience for your partner? If so, how?

What have you learned about the most effective ways to support your partner?

What strategies have been working really well? Not so well?

Is there any additional support or help that you feel would help you to be more effective in this role?

Would you like to continue in this role in the future? Why or why not?

Are there other things you would like to do with your partner?

What makes someone a member of this class?

How do other students in the classroom understand your role as a peer support?

Sources: Bond and Castagnera (2003); Copeland et al. (2004); Hughes et al. (2001); Jones (2007); Kamps et al. (1998); Williams and Downing (1998).

Peer Support Strategies for Improving All Students' Social Lives and Learning
by Erik W. Carter, Lisa S. Cushing, & Craig H. Kennedy
Copyright © 2009 by Paul H. Brookes Publishing Co. All rights reserved.

Reflection Questions for Paraprofessionals and Educators

Person filling out this form: _____ Semester: _____

What has been your overall reaction to implementing peer support strategies?

How would you describe the experiences of students who are participating in these arrangements?

How effective have peers been at providing academic support to their classmates with severe disabilities? Social support?

Are there strategies that peers still need to learn that would make them more effective at supporting their classmates?

What role have peers played in contributing to an inclusive classroom or school?

What concerns do you have about implementing peer support arrangements in your classroom?

(continued)

Sources: Copeland, McCall, et al. (2002); Cushing et al. (1997); Hughes and Carter (2008); Janney, Snell, Beers, and Raynes (1995); York and Tundidor (1995).

Peer Support Strategies for Improving All Students' Social Lives and Learning
by Erik W. Carter, Lisa S. Cushing, & Craig H. Kennedy
Copyright © 2009 by Paul H. Brookes Publishing Co. All rights reserved.

What sort of assistance would be most helpful for you?

In your opinion, what have been the benefits of peer support arrangements to students with disabilities? To their classmates without disabilities? To the peers participating in the peer support initiatives? To school staff?

What aspects of inclusion have been most challenging for you?

What additional informational, resource, or training needs do you have related to including students with severe disabilities in your classroom?

Do you have specific concerns about some aspect of peer support arrangements?

Will you continue to use peer support arrangements in this classroom in the future? How about in other classrooms?

Sources: Copeland, McCall, et al. (2002); Cushing et al. (1997); Hughes and Carter (2008); Janney, Snell, Beers, and Raynes (1995); York and Tundidor (1995).

 Peer Support Strategies for Improving All Students' Social Lives and Learning
by Erik W. Carter, Lisa S. Cushing, & Craig H. Kennedy
Copyright © 2009 by Paul H. Brookes Publishing Co. All rights reserved.

Index

Page references followed by *f* and *t* indicate figures and tables, respectively.